THE C

Charles

In the 21st century, when urbanization is reaching its limits, the population suddenly slumps . . .

The city is killing man

– strangling and crushing humanity as effectively as the jungle destroyed the civilizations of the past.

The characters – zombies, slum-dwellers, a pop star, and an architect – move like tiny insects through the vast empty steel and concrete landscape of the city.

The Loners decide to opt out of civilization . . .
The Civics dare not venture beyond the city limits . . .

which will survive?

THE CITY DWELLERS

To
J. G. Ballard
and
Stephen Black
not forgetting Jailer Mick, Binks, Fred Carpet,
Dave and the rest at 325A.

The City Dwellers

CHARLES PLATT

SPHERE BOOKS LIMITED
30/32 Gray's Inn Road, London, WC1X 8JL

First published in Great Britain in 1970 by Sidgwick & Jackson

First Sphere Books edition, 1971

TRADE
MARK

Set in Linotype Baskerville

Printed in Great Britain by
Hazell Watson & Viney Ltd
Aylesbury, Bucks

PART ONE

TOMORROW PEOPLE

The hotel lounge was crammed full of newsmen and the air was thick and heavy and hot. Loud voices mingled with beat music playing in the background. The people were moving and pressing, tense-faced, eyes and teeth flashing in the video light glare. Greg was the focus; he was surrounded.

'Your first number took how long to work out?' the journalist was shouting, pushing his video machine in Greg's face. Greg answered automatically, leaning up against the wall to stop himself falling over, and talking through the muzziness in his head. 'After a one-niter. Two hours, maybe . . .'

'Future plans?'

The bright shapes and the dazzling lights. The noise and the pressure. Hearing fuzzy.

'Our—our future plans . . .'

A strong hand gripped his arm and pulled him sideways through the pressing bodies. 'Easy now. He's had a rough time, gentlemen. Got to rest for the show tonight. Conference is over. No I'm sorry, finished. No more interviews and no exceptions. It's *over*.'

Greg let himself be towed through the crowd. The faces moved in front of him, still shouting questions. The video lights followed him across the lounge.

And then he was in the next room and the door was locked behind him.

Greg grinned weakly. 'You always time it right, Owen.'

Beside him the heavy-built manager shrugged. 'Wouldn't be worth my twenty per cent if I didn't.'

This room was clearer and cooler with only a few small groups of people standing holding drinks, talking casually; celebrities in the tomorrow music business, sophisticatedly restrained in manner and dress. The newsmen were thumping on the door but no one paid any attention.

Still dazed, Greg let Owen guide him across to a bar at one side of the high-ceilinged, thick-carpeted room. Acquaintances smiled and nodded as he passed.

Owen ordered drinks and dropped two capsules into Greg's glass, watching them dissolve in a spray of orange bubbles. He handed the glass to Greg. 'Sort out your senses. Be right for the concert tonight.'

Greg drank it. He grimaced. 'A month back I'd have faced up to it in there. I'd have had the guts.' He looked up at Owen's heavy features, ugly, shrewd-eyed, thick-wrinkled. What the man lacked in intelligence he made up for with hard common sense. He was dependable.

'I seen this coming, Greg. You're tired, you need a break. That's all. It happens to anyone. I've been making arrangements. There's tonight's show and the one the day after tomorrow. A photo session in between. Get through that, and then you can take a week off, go where you like, do what you want. I'll fix it.'

Greg leant against the bar, staring across the lounge. 'That's fine, Owen. A vacation. Great. But with some creepy sub-teen? Or on my own?'

Owen smiled. He looked smug. He took Greg's arm. 'Over here, I'll give you an intro.'

Greg put down his empty glass. 'Set it all up for me, have you?'

The girl was standing to one side of the room, on her own. She looked twenty-five—six years older then Greg. Long blonde hair with a shimmer of mauve, dark purple dress to the neck with two side slits, conservative but nice. A model's face but with character. She looked intelligent. Unusual.

'Greg, meet Cathy.' Owen turned to the girl. 'Greg's been having a rough time. Maybe he needs a soothing touch.' She smiled briefly at the heavy-built manager. He nodded, walked away.

'I've been waiting to meet you,' said Cathy.

Greg smiled faintly. 'Owen likes to set up situations for me.' He paused, looking closely at her. 'You're in fashion?'

She looked amused. 'Freelance journalist. Nothing glamorous. But I'm off duty, I don't want an interview.'

'No journalist is ever off duty.'

This time, she looked uncomfortable.

Greg glanced at his wrist watch. 'Like a meal? Then my concern, later on?'

There was a small moment's hesitation. 'All right,' she said.

Greg took her arm and they left the room.

It was cool and fresh out in the street. Greg helped her into his car and slammed the door. It was a U.S. turbine import, sleek and sinister with a hunched up rounded look, ready to spring forward. The windows were narrow slits in the blending curves of the steel body shell. It was dusk; the car glinted in the street lights.

Moving out of town on the elevated road the lights of other traffic blinked red and amber in the evening greyness. The engine murmured, wind swept past. He tuned in a U.S. satellite relay music programme; sounds filled the rich snug car interior. He relaxed in the deep, moulded upholstery. 'Hell, they're playing our new number,' he said.

'You've really made it,' she said. Her voice was quiet and relaxed.

He glanced at her. She wasn't looking at him. 'Yes. I have.'

'Right sound, right image. Three months?'

'Two.' He shrugged irritably. 'You didn't want an interview, remember?'

Unexpectedly she laughed. 'I'm sorry. Just reminding myself who I was talking to.'

The music on the radio ended. The deejay cut in. 'It's *it*, it's *IT*, so beautiful you haven't got it you got to get it yeah you *got* to get it baby baby what a *fantastic* tomorrow sound from the boy who *is* tomorrow sound need I say more except get it get it now from your music merchant and girls while you're there grab Allure—Allure eyeglitter for that distinctive bright sparkle the only eyeglitter medically certified does *not* interfere with natural delicate moisture of your eyes. Even soothes tired eyes, makes the men come your way and now I just gotta do this, people, it's so groovy I just gotta play it one more time, tomorrow people, the smash-mash-smash from . . .'

Cathy leant forward and switched it off. 'I hope you don't mind.'

'You want the music, you have to take the plugs.'

'Then perhaps we can do without the music.'

He shrugged.

They soared across a flyover, flashing past cars in the slow lanes, headlight beams sweeping the road. Ahead the moon hung low in skyline haze; near to it the bright star of the abandoned Russian orbital station was a reminder of the moon boom aftermath. Only the cosmats and some pre-seventies unmanned probes were left orbiting in space now, still sending in signals to the last remaining tracking station at Cape Kennedy, museum of the space age.

'Where are we eating?' Cathy asked, breaking the silence. They were still on the elevated road, cutting between roof-tops of one of the slum zones.

Greg smiled thinking on the affairs he'd started this way at the same café. Throw a girl off balance, eat cheap in a poor district like it's what all the tomorrow people do to be different and she didn't know it. She's put at a disadvantage; you move in.

'There's a small café I know. It's really the only way to get away. Simple food, simple people. Maybe you'll like it.'

She smiled easily. So natural and confident all the time, as if she'd be happy with anything that came her way, just took it as it came. It interested him.

They filtered off the highway and down an exit ramp into the slum zone. Two streetlights out of three were smashed. Rubbish littered the road. The houses were dark windowed and shabby. He drove slowly turning from street to street and finally stopping outside a dimly lit corner café.

'You won't believe it, but I used to live three blocks from here.'

'Before things happened for you, you mean?'

'That's right.'

'I didn't know that.'

'Not many do.' He turned off the ignition. 'Hope this is O.K. for you, Cathy.'

She nodded. 'Refreshing to find something really different.'

They sat by the window, eating off old china plates on a wooden table with a faded check cloth that wasn't quite big enough. The window was filmed with condensation; drab pot plants stood on the sill. Service was intermittent; the place was almost empty but the waiter spent a lot of time talking to friends at another table and there was some kind of family argument going on in the kitchen. Men and women in ragged clothes shuffled in occasionally and collected meals to take away – greasy paper bags of food they held tight as if to keep their hands warm. Greg and Cathy were ignored.

'People forget the slums,' Greg said. 'There's so much happening in the city. But thousands are living poor. Isolated, left to themselves.'

'In what way?'

'See, it's like this: no one has money here, so the big companies don't angle any advertising this way. The whole zone's unexploited, because it has nothing to give.'

'You really once lived here?'

'Till a year ago. I came here to make it on my own. It's the cheapest living there is. But the longer I lived here the more I fitted in. So relaxed, great sense of community. When you're poor and so is everyone else it makes you stick together. Real friendships.'

She smiled. 'You don't fit in here now.'

He looked away from her, out of the window. 'If that's

so, I guess I'm glad. I could have stagnated here. Like most of the others. I might have bummed around all my life and never tried anything. Most people here end up that way.'

'Maybe they're happy that way.'

'If they are, it's because they haven't had a chance to feel what it's like to make it out in real life.'

She looked at her hands on the table. 'That sounds hollow to me, Greg.'

He turned and stared at her a moment. 'Don't try cross examining me, all right?' he said angrily.

She looked at her watch. 'What time are we due at your concert?'

There was a short, awkward silence. He pulled out some money and put it on the table, then looked at his watch. 'We're late,' he said. 'Hell, Owen'll be mad. You shouldn't have got me talking so much, like that.' He pushed back his chair and got up.

She didn't say anything. They hurried out; no one in the café bothered to look up as they left.

Total Experience

They reached the theatre fifteen minutes before Greg was due on stage. Owen was waiting at the stage door. Police with riot clubs were holding the girls back.

Greg got as far as possible with the car. The girls were packed solid blocking the road. 'Don't get out till the crowd's dispersed,' Greg shouted to Cathy. Screaming from outside submerged his words. 'They'll tear you apart. Wait for Owen. He'll fix things for you.'

The young faces crowded forward contorted and shouting, crying, reaching, sharp-eyed, and wanting. Greg fumbled with the door catch not wanting to go out there, but the longer he left it the more the girls pushed forward and the police cordon gave ground. The gangway to the stage door was narrowing. Owen was in the doorway shouting something but Greg couldn't hear.

He lunged out of the car shielding his face with his hands. Sound and colour hit him and the smell of girls' perfume mingling with dust and sweat raised by thousands of pressing bodies rolled over him in suffocating waves. Hands, hands, stretching and grabbing for him. High-pitched screaming, surging and fading but coming at him from all directions, echoing off the buildings. He pushed through blundering blindly, hair and skin torn by fingernails. The police cordon gave way a little, a little more, then suddenly it collapsed. The girls pressed forward. Greg panicked, fell on his hands and lunged up again through forests of trampling legs, girls fighting for him, trying to scratch, grab, bite, pull, tear, cut, devour him. Somehow Owen waded out through the mass and grabbed him forward through the tide of young bodies, breasts, faces, hands, eyes, nails and teeth.

And suddenly he was inside. Clothes torn, hands bloody. Owen slammed the heavy metal door shouting '. . . an hour ago! Christ we got ten minutes to get the TE make-up on you rig the sound gear . . .'

Greg stumbled dazed following Owen through passages up stairs to the dressing room. Inside it ten young women in clean blue overalls turned like a formation, ready to apply skin tone, hair colour, foundation paste and flesh sculpt to mould Greg into his image.

He slumped into the makeup chair and the small yellow-walled room closed in round him. Fingers gently sponged his face, undid his torn clothes, soothed cuts, and covered blemishes and bruises. They started building up the tints and colourings. They added and accentuated the contours of his skin. The women worked as a team, never speaking, tending to the idol they were creating with their hands. Greg shut his eyes and let it happen.

Five minutes later they finished and quietly left the room. He opened his eyes and saw himself in the mirror. The plastic flesh they'd added accentuated his face's hard, aggressively sexual lines. Eye colouring had blackened the irises, whitened the whites. Spray tinting had highlighted the natural contrasts of face tone. He bared his 'pure-white' teeth, looked down at his flared scarlet clothes. He was suddenly beautiful.

'You can talk now,' Owen said. 'The flesh sculpt will have set.'

Greg stood up feeling shaky. 'Sorry I was late, that girl, Cathy got me talking . . . Find her a seat, Owen. Somewhere near the stage. Where I can see her and she can see me.'

Backstage, the sound was overpowering. Technicians, earmuffled, bent over consoles synchronizing the total experience equipment, mixing sound, colour, and odour. Greg waited while Owen strapped on the subvocal microphone under his collar and an engineer tested the circuits. A girl touched up his makeup and smoothed his suit. No one spoke; words were useless against the pounding, clamouring noise. The concrete floor was vibrating underfoot.

Greg smiled. The nervous exhilaration, slightly trembling hands, hot skin of his face . . . it was all just as it should be. He was going to be good, singing in front of Cathy.

He ignored the other feeling. The exhausted, depleted feeling he was giving something over and over again which he couldn't go on giving to audiences of girls that never stopped taking. He was tired, he knew that, but the feeling was more than the kind of tiredness a vacation could cure. Somehow, it was almost sexual . . .

Then the noise ended. Technicians snapped off controls on the consoles and threaded new programme tapes. The preceding singer came offstage, sweating, limp and drained of everything. Greg waited. Soon he'd be out all alone.

The compere was racing through the intro. No one listened, everyone was screaming. Owen nodded and Greg walked onstage behind the still-closed curtains. In the wings, technicians gave him the O.K. signal.

The stage was white, horse-shoe shaped, backed by a giant Diacora depth-effect back-projection screen, a shimmering white curtain like an untouched canvas. Greg stood in the centre, waiting.

Then the intro was over and the curtains parted and Greg was face to face with the audience, a wall of human colour hazy behind the spotlights, rippling mass of young girls open mouthed and screaming, hungry and demanding. The music blasted out from a battery of sound panels above the stage and Greg walked forward buffeted by sound and colour, moving instinctively to the music. Behind him the screen lit up in an exploding barrage of depth images, swirling and shimmering, merging and blending as the clamour of the music increased. Then he started singing and simultaneously his face emerged from the colours on the screen behind and either side of him, magnified several hundred times. TE cameras mounted up by the spotlights zeroed on him and behind him his features grew until his eyes and mouth filled the entire vast screen, moving as he moved, contorted with emotion, radiating sex, want, hate, lust, power. Giant fans wafted waves of heady masculine odour over the audience. Colours flashed in synchronized patterns, shifting with the music that drowned even the screaming. The whole structure of the concert hall trembled.

Early on he glimpsed Cathy in the third row watching him sober-faced and quiet, with the writhing, shouting, sobbing sub-teens all round her. But then Greg lost himself to the total experience, sounds and smells and colours, no longer thinking, drowning in the music and emotion pounding on all sides. Dust and noise and sweat on his face, feeling it raw under the lights, ten thousand screams lifting him up, cutting him off, draining him.

Afterwards, like always, was like stepping out of technicolour into monochrome. The newsmen closed in on him. He tried to focus his eyes, to hear through deadened ears. His skin was numb, his mouth was dry, he was covered in sweat. The backstage room was drab and badly lit and he shivered in his crumpled red clothes despite the close, heavy atmosphere. He answered their questions and forced a smile while inside he slowly started coming back to reality.

As soon as he could he got away, peeled off his makeup and changed into fresh clothes. Cathy had waited for him; he found her and managed to leave the crowds behind.

'I'll take you home,' he said dully, feeling weak and out of touch. The stage experience had been altogether too orgasmic.

He took her hand and they went down a flight of concrete stairs and along a dim, yellow-walled corridor. 'There's an underground garage. We'll drive out that way; maybe some of the crowds will have gone home.'

'You were almost killed by that mob, on the way in.'

'Don't talk about it,' he said.

The car was waiting ready; they drove up and out of the exit ramp, edging through a small crowd of girls trying to cling to the car as it passed. Then they were out in the evening city traffic. Greg said little, driving slowly with the traffic, hardly noticing the vehicles in front, mechanically following Cathy's route directions to get to her apartment building.

Her block stood at the top of a hill, tall and square in shiny tinted concrete. He double parked in the wide street lined with expensive buildings and continental cars.

For a moment he sat listening to the murmur of the idling car engine and the rhythm of the passing traffic.

'I'd never been to a total experience show before,' she said. 'I'd only read about them.'

He looked across at her. 'Did you like it?'

She looked at her hands in her lap. 'Put it this way, Greg. I grew up with pop music when there were groups, it was simple, maybe a few lights, the music was live instead of taped, it wasn't so staged. Loud, but not overwhelming. There wasn't the personality cult, the calculated hysteria . . .'

'What are you trying to say? You didn't like my act?'

She glanced at him, then quickly away. 'I'm sorry, Greg.

I can see you're good at it. The best, probably. But not for me. Maybe it's just I'm—I'm too old. The kids there were all twelve, thirteen . . . For me, it was too much. Too much *everything.*'

He shrugged. 'That's what people want. The rest of the audience liked me, even if you didn't.'

'You talk as if your stage image was *you,* Greg. That's ridiculous.'

He frowned, then sighed, shaking his head. 'Maybe you're right. Maybe . . . Hell, I'm tired, it took too much out of me this time, it doesn't matter that much whether you liked my act.'

'I don't know how you can go on giving out to audiences that way, every night.'

He said nothing.

'Sometimes I got the feeling, all they really wanted was to rip you to pieces.'

He closed his eyes. 'When you make it, everyone wants a piece . . .' The conversation died. But she still sat quietly, waiting. Eventually Greg looked out at the street and the houses. 'You live well,' he said.

For a moment she seemed disconcerted. 'I was born into it.'

He waited but she didn't go on. He turned and they looked at each other; he reached out, touching her hand, caressing her arm under her plastic coat sleeve. He leant across the car's instrument console and touched her cheek gently with his other hand, feeling the softness of her skin under the makeup. They kissed moist and gently and he breathed her scent and felt the gentleness of her against him, rustling her clothes. He kissed eyes-open, watching her face, lit one side by the streetlights. He kissed her harder, touching the smooth skin of her thighs above the spray-on stockings; but it was a routine, not an impulse, and she drew back a little.

'You must be tired,' she said. Her voice made him suddenly relax. At once he realized, there were no obligations on him this time. She expected nothing.

'I'd like to see you tomorrow afternoon,' he said at last, not knowing what to feel.

'That's fine.'

'Two o'clock?'

She nodded.

He kissed her again briefly and then she got out of the car, calm, and graceful, walking quickly over to her apartment block. Greg watched her open the door of the building and disappear inside. It was as if she knew too much about him and he knew nothing of her. Suddenly it was he who was at a disadvantage, and he didn't know how it had happened. She was so very cool about it all.

CATHY

From her top floor apartment Cathy looked out over the whole city, spread in a wide panorama of lights as far as the haze-softened horizon. She undressed slowly in front of her big bedroom window, letting the clothes fall on the carpet, soft and warm under her bare feet.

She walked to the long wardrobe and ran her hand over the expensive dresses inside, watching the rich fabrics shimmer in the low room lighting. The smell of the expensive clothes mingled with her own perfume. She breathed in deeply, tilting her head back so her hair tickled her shoulders, and ran the palms of her hands down over her smooth body.

Still naked she turned and fell face down on her wide bed. The tufted quilt pressed up against her firm body. It felt good against her skin.

Luxury never ceased to delight her. She didn't seem capable of becoming tired of living well. But even as she thought about it, she felt the familiar discontent creeping into her mind.

She turned on her side, staring at the darkness outside her window. She thought of Greg, his energy, his youngness. Young in every way. But refreshing after the endless succession of professional businessmen obsessed with their careers, worried about their waistlines, their creeping baldness, their virility. Too many men, exhausted at thirty-five, dull minded and looking for a woman to console them and reassure them, while they offered her nothing.

Greg would be different. He had what the others lacked. He could please her in the way they couldn't.

Or maybe she was fooling herself again. She doubted everything, herself, her men, her life. What was there to believe in?

The thought patterns were not new. They never led anywhere. Best not to think, best to let it happen, like she had that night. Act as if Greg was going to be everything.

Open Skies

The day was bright and hot and the city looked good in the sun, people hurrying on the pavements, buildings baking in the heat. Greg drove with the car top slid back, not hurrying, taking time to look around. The streets had a used, dusty smell that mingled with the smell of the people and the exhaust fumes from the traffic. Greg liked the smell, he liked belonging to a city where everyone was busy, knew what was happening, wearing tomorrow clothes and doing what was new. Doctors still talked of city life being unhealthy for mind and body. Emotional pressures. Suicide statistics. Lung cancer. Hospital records. Doctors had always talked that way. Greg ignored them. What mattered was now and here in the centre, setting tastes and interacting with everyone else, surrounded by the people and the tower blocks, the lights and traffic. It was part of Greg, and of all the millions like him – others not so successful, not so much at the focus of things, but just as much caught by the pace of city living. In a way Greg represented them all. He was them and they were him.

Cathy's block was an hour's drive from the centre – too far for Greg's taste. There were trees on the pavement and the buildings were spaced apart, set back from the road. It was more like a suburb than part of the city.

He was early so he grabbed a parking space outside her building and sat waiting in the car, watching the scene outside. People were richly dressed but a month out of style, typically suburb. Cathy had better taste.

He saw the entrance door of her block swing open but it was a man who came out. He wore a stained, crumpled raincoat and moved awkwardly as if embarrassed by his shabby outfit. He glanced quickly behind him before hurrying down the road, hunched forward holding his coat tightly around him. Greg turned and watched. There was something wrong with the man's arms; he held them close to his body stiffly, like rigid sticks.

He forgot about the man when Cathy came out five minutes later. She was smiling, eyes alive, wearing a to-morrow dress with a front slit showing slices of her body as she moved. She kissed hello, lips a tiny bit sticky from fresh tinting. Her breath was faintly peppermint.

'You look even better than yesterday,' he said.

'Because it's a sunny day. Let's get out to the country-side, Greg.'

He paused a second. 'You really want me to?'

'Sure. Who needs sunshine in the city?'

He shrugged. 'All right.'

Their eyes met. Cathy put her hand on his. 'Greg, I want to do what you want. What is it, have you planned something else?'

He shook his head. 'Forget it. You're right, it's a countryside day. I'm just a city dweller, so much in town I forget there's anything outside it.' He put the car into drive and moved out into the traffic stream, not looking at her.

She shot him a doubting glance, then sat back into her seat, tossing her long hair behind her.

'There's a houseboat and launch I've got on a river thirty miles out,' Greg went on. 'Owen bought it a couple of months back but I've never used it. Secluded. Is that all right for you?'

'Yes.' Her voice was flat and dull.

The traffic slowed and stopped. Greg held the car on the brake and looked at her, frowning. 'What's wrong?'

She turned. 'Don't make sacrifices, that's all, Greg. It'd spoil things.' She looked suddenly serious.

The traffic was moving again. Greg gripped the steering and accelerated into a faster traffic lane. He didn't answer what Cathy had said. He didn't want to make any sacrifices, either. He shouldn't be driving her out of town when he didn't want to. She wasn't that important, was she? How had she got to him so strongly, so soon? But hell, there was no point thinking about it. Couldn't turn back now. Make something out of things as they were. When he got out there he might even enjoy it.

It was a long, tough drive. City sub-centres one after another with their industries, overspill, traffic problems, shopping centre detours. Greg was edgy by the time they finally broke free of the built-up zones. He blasted past the rest of the traffic and hit a hundred and ten, forgetting the speed restriction signs. The engine roared and the car vibrated and the air rushed past making Cathy's hair stream out behind her. The speed was so good, it was like power injected into his body; when he looked at Cathy it made him feel even better.

They slowed and turned off the main road and through narrow sun-and-shade country lanes, tall hedges flashing past, car tyres scattering gravel. 'Only been here once before, when Owen first set it up. He took over moorings half a mile each way up and down the river so it'd stay private.'

Greg slowed and turned the car off the road into a gravelled clearing big enough for two cars. Beams of afternoon sun slanted down through the thick, tall trees all round. Insects hummed in the shadows.

They got out of the car. 'This track leads down to the boat. I'd take the car down but it's built too low to clear the bumps. We'll have to walk.'

She took her shoes off. 'I like walking.'

The river was at the bottom of the long slope. Cathy ran down to it uninhibited and free, unzipping her dress and letting it fall in the grass. She had a bikini underneath; she ran straight off the bank into the river. Greg watched, smiling.

She swam back and crawled out, hair stuck wet to her head and shoulders.

'Greg, it's marvellous.'

She stood on the bank, skin beaded with water, and stared up at the empty sky, wriggling her toes in the grass. She shook her wet hair out of her face, looked at him and kissed him on tiptoe, arms around his neck.

'Undress. We'll swim together.'

He shook his head. 'No. But you go ahead.'

She turned and jumped in the water again. Greg glanced round him at the rich green vegetation, bushes and trees, tall grass and brambles. He sighed, wondering what was bringing him down so much.

He walked to the small hover launch and started taking the covers off, while she splashed around in the water. 'Come and put on these water skis,' he called.

Soon he was towing her up and down the river, the little launch bouncing over its own wake and Cathy riding the skis in showers of spray catching rainbows in the clear sunlight. The air was bright and fresh. Undergrowth lined the banks, patterning the water with shifting shadows. Greg felt happy to see her happy.

But countryside was such a drag. The sun was already burning him, making him sweat-sticky and lethargic. His head had started to ache. When he stopped the motor of the launch, the silence was overpowering.

Later they lay together in the sun side by side on the bank. Greg held her to him, kissing her, enjoying their firm bodies side by side. 'Happy?' he asked.

'Very happy.' Her eyes were alive and exciting and he wished he could feel closer to her and less detached. The heat; maybe that's what had sapped his energy.

Gently he undid her bikini top and slid it off her. He

touched her smooth breasts and kissed them. She lay back on the grass under him, lips parted, breathing a little fast.

'Let's go . . . into the houseboat,' he said. 'It'll be cooler, more comfortable. And private.'

She shook her head. 'No. Here, in the open.'

'But we could be seen, or . . .'

She just pulled him down to her and slid her hands inside his shirt, stroking his skin and holding him close to her. He smiled faintly and kissed her with increasing desire, undoing the other half of her bikini while she pulled his shirt off and loosened his trousers.

When they were naked she pressed herself hard against him, wanting him to make love to her, but he found it so hard to feel right with her and give himself like he should. The ground was hard and the sun was hot on his back. He felt exposed, going through the motions of exciting her, detached, as if watching himself.

Why didn't it come naturally?

She was gasping and crying as they moved together but too soon what passion he'd managed to find died away, and he pulled back feeling angry, seeing her disappointed.

'I'm sorry,' he said.

She tried to smile. Gently her hand closed round his weak, limp penis.

'I can help,' she said.

She was incredibly gentle, soft and kind as if nursing him back to life. She restored a little of the feeling. She tried so hard he couldn't bear it.

'It's not going to work,' he said, wanting to be anywhere but close beside her. 'Leave it. Can't we leave it? Try some other time. There'll be other times.'

Immediately she was holding herself close to him, looking up at him. 'Of course,' she said. She bit her lip. 'It was my fault, making you, out here when you wanted . . . do you still want to, in the houseboat?'

He shook his head. He pulled a little free from her, embarrassed by her closeness. 'It doesn't normally happen like this with me,' he lied.

'It's all right. It really is. Men don't realize how often

this kind of thing happens, they expect it to be perfect every time. But most of the men I've known in the last few years – businessmen, city workers – when they get home, perhaps it's because they're tired, depleted. They won't admit it, they talk a lot about virility and sex . . .'

She trailed off, looking away from him.

He lay a little longer on the grass beside her. He didn't want to think about it. But he couldn't help wondering why he felt so indifferent, and why there was even a feeling of relief, like being free from obligation. Like in the car when he'd taken her home the previous night. For no reason his thoughts jumped back to the girls outside the theatre mobbing him, their faces contorted, mouths gaping, hands scrabbling for him. Always people wanting him.

His thoughts were broken by the distant buzzing of his car radiophone. He jumped up and dragged on his trousers, running quickly up the gravel slope leaving Cathy by the river.

Owen's face was on the screen. 'Tonight's photographic session, Greg. It's been moved forward an hour. And beforehand I want to fix your vacation details. Hotel reservations, airline bookings.'

'When do you need me?'

'Soon as you can. Where are you now?'

'The river. With Cathy. It'll take an hour back to town, another hour from her place to yours.'

'Then we'll meet half way. There's a hotel near Cathy's place – the Queen Anne. Meet you in the bar at five. She'll tell you where it is.'

'Right.'

Greg broke the connection. So Owen knew where Cathy lived. He hadn't thought to find out what the link was between the two of them. It might be interesting if Owen knew other things about the girl.

He ran back down the path and found Cathy getting into her dress.

'We have to go now?' she asked.

Greg shrugged. 'Business.' Quickly he put the covers on

the launch and dressed. She watched him with a sad smile.

'You're impatient to get back to town, aren't you?' she said.

He hardly noticed her. 'I've got to,' he said.

The drive back was dull and tiring and they sat in silence most of the way. He knew he should say something. She was unhappy and it was his fault, and he ought to care, but he didn't. Too much effort, so much easier to think about driving and forget about any obligations toward her.

He parked outside her apartment block and she told him how to find the hotel where he was meeting Owen. He looked at her and knew she was wondering why he was being so cold. But it was yet another demand. What did she want from him, anyway?

'Don't worry about this afternoon,' she said. 'I understand.'

He tried to kiss her warmly but couldn't tell whether he had or not.

She smiled quickly. 'See you again?' she said. She looked as if she was wondering if he'd still be interested in her. He looked at her face and the sight of her softened some of his indifference. She was so unusual. She could get through to him in a way that really disturbed him.

'Maybe we could meet tomorrow,' he said.

She nodded. 'Yes. Phone me.'

She opened the door to get out. 'I enjoyed this afternoon in spite of everything.'

He didn't answer. She slammed the car door.

Failures

The hotel was only minutes away. Greg left his car in the car park and found the bar Owen had mentioned. It was wide, low-ceilinged, dim-lit and hot – the air was heavy, suffocating. The furnishings were plush. The place was packed.

Greg pushed his way through the crowds, looking for Owen.

The women all wore heavy make-up, synthetically sexy in provocative clothes. They stood aggressively sexy, sharp eyed. Their teeth were bright white against tinted lips.

The men were loud and trying to be impressive in tight black and dark red suits flared in extravagant styles. But their lazy postures and hesitant, limp mannerisms didn't match their fashions. The pretentiousness was bold but hollow.

Few people recognized Greg, and those that did couldn't quite place his face. His fans and followers were strictly sub-teen.

He searched through the whole bar but couldn't find Owen. He chewed his thumb nail impatiently and tried to get across to the quieter end where there was some space to stand, away from the crush of people. But he got caught up in a moving mass of women, shoving him suddenly to one side so he stumbled off balance and fell awkwardly against one of the small round tables, knocking someone's glass off and on to the floor, splashing the drink over himself and the stranger at the table.

He caught his balance, dabbed at the stains on his trousers, glanced at the man sitting at the table and started a routine apology. But then he stopped and frowned, realizing the man's face was familiar. It was the same shabby figure in the grey raincoat who Greg had seen that afternoon, walking out of Cathy's apartment block.

'Sorry about that, friend,' he said. 'I'll buy you another.'

The man shook his head quickly. He had paste-grey skin, receding hair, pale grey eyes. A missing tooth. He needed a shave.

He sat tense and edgy, his hands trembling slightly as they lay on the table. 'That's quite all right,' he said in a thin, reedy voice. 'Not your fault. I saw how it happened, think nothing . . .'

'No, I insist.' Greg snatched up the man's glass, avoiding his futilely grasping hand, and filled it from the nearest coindrop dispenser, choosing the best brand.

'It was you I saw, leaving Cathy's place this afternoon, wasn't it?' he asked casually, picking up another glass and filling it for himself.

The man started, looking up nervously. 'Have you been watching me or something?'

Greg laughed easily. He set the two glasses on the table and sat down beside the man. 'Not at all. I was visiting, happened to notice you. You know Cathy?'

A nervous tic twitched under the man's prominent cheekbone. 'I . . . well, yes, I know someone called Cathy.'

'I'll introduce myself. Greg Anderson, beat singer, you may have heard the name.'

The man's face twitched again. 'Pleased to meet . . . that is, my name's Jamieson. I won't shake hands, if you don't mind.' As he spoke the involuntary tremor in his arm increased without warning, rattling against the table top. He looked embarrassed. 'I'd better explain, I have artificial arms.' He hit one arm with his fist. There was the thump of plastic on plastic. 'Thalidomide case. Always causes trouble. I was one of the first . . .'

Greg's expression was immediately one of concern. 'Terrible.'

'It does get me down. Cathy . . .'

'You do know her, then?'

'I'm an old friend of hers, you might say. Yes, an old friend. You?'

'Close friend.'

'I see. Yes, I see. Well, I'm married myself. Cathy, well she cheers me up sometimes, you might say. I, that is, my wife's divorcing me. Cathy's good company. Nice girl. Wouldn't you say?' He looked up as if for reassurance. Greg nodded, unconvinced. Jamieson was hiding something.

The man lit a cigarette with awkward, jerky movements that he tried to hide by pulling his arms in close to his dirty raincoat. His face was rigid with nervous tension.

'Tell me about yourself,' Greg said.

'I'm . . . sociologist, unemployed.' Jamieson smiled inanely as if he'd made a joke; the next moment, his features collapsed. 'Shouldn't mumble on this way but it's not as if I often talk to people, you must excuse . . . I was at university, you know, till it got to be too much for me. Having psychiatric treatment now but it's not enough, never enough, State sponsored you understand, they can't afford to spend too much on people of no productive value, know what I mean?' He drank deeply from his glass. It rattled momentarily against his teeth. Greg suddenly knew, instinctively, the man wore dentures.

Jamieson was half drunk and getting worse. His face warped into a new expression as he put his glass down. His mouth stretched out as if tensing to keep the words inside; but then they tumbled out. 'R . . . R . . . Research. My research got on top of me. Damn it I always end up telling people. Like a bloody missionary spreading the truth.' Again the inane laughter. 'Researching into population, first. Looking for reasons behind the fluctuations. Why's it fashionable to have large families one century, not the next? Always factors you can't pin down. No one really knows the real reason why. Fertility fluctuations, psychological factors. Research was a dead end but it made me face things.'

'What?'

Jamieson gestured erratically around him. 'What? Everything. People. We get so used to it, the overcrowding, population still rising, people pressing close all the time. They talked about it a lot in the sixties, but we're *feeling* it now. Still people don't see how it produces pressures – eat, buy, consume, hurry, the whole consumerism business. Racing to keep productivity up because everything's running short. Resources depleted, so raw materials cost more. People living longer and more of them, they have to be supported. Food problems; not enough of anything. Because of fertility, get it? Fertility. Babies. Women. Sex.

'Now the future. No time, no money, no men left these days for research. No more space programmes, atomic physics, biochemistry, radio astronomy. It's all channelled into feeding, housing, caring for people. New cities – the linear cities being built all over anticipating the next baby boom. Stagnation everywhere else. Oh, everyone talks new – advertising, the rest. But it's all variations on old themes. The old consumerism economics, forces us . . .'

'I've heard this all before,' Greg cut in through the man's ramblings. 'On TV, in magazines, people like you, predicting the end of it all. They always have, always will. You don't realize, things are better than they've ever been. Life's better. Fuller. Richer.'

Jamieson angrily grabbed Greg's jacket. His plastic fingers clicked together. 'The advertising, the government news bulletins, they all make you think that. It might have been true ten years ago. But not now. Everything's running dry, now. Soon, too many people for the resources. But before then, it'll be all over. The pressures – breed, live, hurry, buy – it tires you out till you don't have anything to give any more. Marriage is killed. Everyone's used up. The pressures; they kill love, life, sex, you can't give.'

Greg stood up suddenly. 'You're drunk, you don't know what . . .'

'Did that get to you? Did that one hurt? I see you, I see the whole population. Like you, all of them. Tomorrow people. Fast and tough but you don't realize, you're all used up like everything else.' Jamieson's face moved in one great spasm. 'You. Me. Dried up. Nothing left . . . nothing left to give.'

Greg stood tense and on the edge of losing control. He tried to be rational. Jamieson knew nothing about him, couldn't see into his private life. What he was saying, it was coincidence . . .

'Let go of me.' He prised the mechanical fingers away. The man slumped down. 'No one listens,' he mumbled.

Greg turned and pushed through the crowds of people. More had come in while he'd been talking. He blundered through the pressure of the richly dressed bodies. All he wanted was to get out into the air.

At the door he stumbled into Owen.

'Greg! Look, I tried to make it, but the bloody traffic, the whole city's jammed, I came by the new monorail link . . .' He turned in surprise as Greg walked past without looking round.

'Greg! What is it? Hell, I'm late, but – is it Cathy? Something wrong?'

Greg reached his car, opened the door and glanced back. 'Leave me alone, Owen. I'd better call you later.'

He got in and shut the door. The roof slid forward and the windows wound up, sealing him in. The engine started with a roar. Owen shouted and gesticulated as Greg revved the engine and accelerated out of the car park.

Slum Dweller

For one unreal moment he'd thought and felt that Jamieson knew all about him, could see right inside to what had happened that afternoon with Cathy. As if the man *knew*. Stupid, but he'd had to get away. From Jamieson, Owen, everyone.

His life hadn't been working right and it wasn't getting better but he didn't know if it was just tiredness or something else as well. Cathy had made it plainer, more obvious so he couldn't ignore it any more, this feeling of wanting but not wanting, not giving, not trying even, though he needed her, he knew that, she was so good, she had so much but it all needed sorting out even though he didn't want even to think about it it only made it worse or maybe it gets worse either way, can't control it, oh fuck oh shit to hell with them and fuck them all, so hard to break free, that holding-pressing-I-can't feeling all the time but so difficult, can't pin it down, let alone control and – damn it, those traffic signals he'd driven straight through on red and could have smashed into that woman back there and, where was he going, anyway?

Back in reality, he saw he'd driven blindly into the

slum zone. He slowed and stopped the car by the kerb in one of the deserted, dirty streets. He turned off the engine and for a long time just sat staring out of the windscreen as dusk fell.

A tenement like that was where it started, stinking damp, leaking lavatory, hell, remember that time at the party the man downstairs coming up shouting there's piss coming through my ceiling – lots of times like that and no one cared a damn it was somehow happy there with the crowd, all of us wanting something better but did it matter and could you ever get it, you needed that first push, first meeting, you needed contacts and no one had anything, too used to living rough and god it really was rough stinking awful waking aching half drugged on cheap pills, rot your guts but got to blot it out sometimes. Not easy to see clearly now how it really was then, bad times and good times, maybe more often it was bad times, but sometimes, well, remember that girl, what was her name she got picked up for carrying didn't she always, was so careless but that night, when it was, she couldn't get enough of it and neither could I, felt so great the next morning tangled up in the sheets, dirty sheets, dirty room but I had my woman . . . so all right, face it, you give up being a slummer, give up being broke, smelly, starving, dirty, you lose *something*, you don't ever get the old we're-all-no-good-bums equality bit again. But what you get instead, the money, the stage act, giving it all out like it's some crazy dream. So why get bugged by Jamieson's crap when it's crap and nothing else, he touched something that was wide open and raw, hell, when I haven't had it properly with a girl for three weeks and it wasn't that good before then, damn it anyone would begin to feel it and Cathy, the way she got through to me, makes it so much worse, maybe if I'd only met her three months back when it was starting to happen and I was making it with those creepy sub-teens to see how many I could have in a night and all that shit, Cathy'd have been good for me then and I'd have been good for her, so now I need her God I need her but how, how can I . . . No, crap, it's been just two days and there's tomorrow, see her then, sort out who Jamieson is, she'll come on my vacation, it's obvious Owen was setting that up from the start, I'll snap out of this mess and it'll happen with Cathy like never before, it can be so good, I know it can. I *know* it can.

He blinked, realizing it was dark outside, wondering how long he'd been sitting there. He stretched, tired and stiff, and started the car. He drove away and up the street, dialling Owen on the radiophone.

His face came on the screen. He looked worried. 'Had to sort things out,' Greg explained, keeping it casual. 'Sorry, Owen. I couldn't stop.'

Owen grunted. 'Where are you now?'

'Elevated road, heading back into town. Where do I meet you?'

Owen gave the address. Greg headed on to the city centre, leaving the slum zone behind him.

Pleasure Palace

The day was grey with rain and the city was alive with wet sounds, raindrops on plastic overcoats, car tyres hissing, gutters splashing, feet tramping through puddles.

The rain rattled on the car roof and spat on the windscreen; the wipers hummed in steady rhythm sweeping over the curved glass.

'The city looks good in the rain,' Greg said.

Sitting beside him, Cathy pulled up her fur coat collar to cover her cheeks and ears. 'I hate wet weather.'

Greg smiled to himself. 'Autumn's coming. Summer's almost over. But I'm taking time off, vacationing in the sun.'

'You're lucky.'

He glanced at her, then away again. 'You could come with me.' He paused. She stayed silent, waiting for him to go on. 'Owen's fixed the details. Five days in the Mediterranean. Starting two days from now.' He glanced at her again. 'Can you make it with me?'

She smiled. 'Thanks for the invitation, but I can't decide now.'

'When?'

'Let me phone you, tonight.'

'What is it, work commitments you've got to go through with? Owen can fix that.'

'It isn't so simple. I have . . . obligations. To friends. I must check with them first.'

It was getting harder to be off-hand. 'You like to keep your life a mystery, don't you? I don't even know what your work is, you never told me.'

'I did. When we met.' She looked away, out of the window at the rain.

Greg laughed sourly. 'Journalist off-duty. You still can't think of anything better than that?'

She was silent for a while. Eventually she spoke, quietly and slowly: 'If you came into my private life now, Greg, you'd change it. And I hardly know you. Why should I alter everything to suit you? Why should you know everything? Not yet.'

He relaxed a little. 'All right. Maybe I was pushing a little too hard.'

He still wanted to know about her – her link with Jamieson, and with Owen. But she was right, there was time.

They drove over a bridge spanning the river, hazy and grey in the rain.

'Where are we going?' Cathy asked.

'Pleasure palace,' Greg said. 'Did you read about it? Opened two weeks back. Fifty acres of delight. Seventeen floors. Under one roof. You must have seen the ads.'

They found the road blocked with traffic approaching the pleasure palace building. It came into view, vast, windowless, bright-painted concrete, straggling over three blocks like tumbled-together cubist foot hills surrounding a central mountain jutting up mis-shapenly in the centre. Slogans and sales messages moved and flashed against the dullness of the sky.

They left the car in a cavernous underground park and took an elevator up. Inside the building the entrance hall was a maze of tilted, moving floors, shifting light curtains, vibrating, pulsing walls, sweeping stairways, and music drifting at random from above, below, and behind. Glowing signs on walls and ceiling listed routes to total experience theatre, cybernet, dream explorer, zero G baths, light rides, think tanks, mind grinders.

Cathy held on to Greg, bewildered by shifting 3D effects and strobe lights calculated to sever reality referents right from the start. Mist rose out of the floor which suddenly turned transparent so they seemed to walk a hundred yards about the Niagara Falls. The floor tilted, and roaring, gushing sounds filled the air. A floor section turned opaque and started sliding to one side, carrying Greg, Cathy, and a group of others through a light curtain.

Suddenly it was dark. Strawberry scented gas hit Greg in the face. He breathed in, coughed, lights came on. As he watched, perspectives distorted, vision swirled and warped, colours intensified. They were moving through an abstract spectrum of light forms projected 3D so it felt almost as if the light moved through one's mind; but the shapes conjured up by the abstract patterns somehow resolved into fantasy figures, nightmare dream images chasing round in increasing horror. Greg shut his eyes, but the patterns on his eyelids were still worse.

Another sharp-smelling gas, and everything turned scarlet. His face flushed, his pulse raced, pleasure exploded, he was drifting in oceans of ecstacy. Then ice blue: now drowning in tears, rending emotion, stomach-sucking grief. And the emotions followed each other through with a kaleidoscope of colours: pain yellow, excitement pink, hilarity green, dour brown, contentment orange, anger red, each sensation resonating with his mind and body, absorbing him totally.

At last the devastating sequence ended. Sharp ammonia-tainted cold air blasted for thirty seconds while it went dark. Emotion subsided, vision stabilized. The lights came on gradually. They were out, somewhere else in the palace.

'It's over?' said Cathy as though she couldn't believe it.

Greg nodded, numb but tingling with elation. Cathy could hardly stand; it had hit her harder.

'Rest a moment,' he said. 'Along here.'

They walked through a narrow snaking passage grotesque with shifting light patterns, through two rippling doors labelled 'Air Baths'.

Inside, the room was washed with shifting blue-green light, fluorescent and depth-effect, rippling up from floor to ceiling like trails of glowing smoke. Greg and Cathy lay down on delineated floor areas and he worked the coinop mechanism. Air jets blasted up through holes in the floor, gently raising Greg and Cathy on cushions of air. Side jets lifted plastic streamers anchored to the floor; the filmy strips rose like sea fronds around each person, shutting out everything but the rippling blue-green ceiling above.

Cathy relaxed; the air cushion adjusted whichever way she turned, supporting her effortlessly until after three minutes it subsided gently and the plastic streamers fluttered down.

Greg helped her up and they wandered into the next pair of doors they saw. Jagged, dissonant sounds and flashing lights blasted out to meet them.

'Let's try something else,' she began, but the door had swung shut behind them. Blinding sheets of white light swept down from the ceiling, the floor jerked and trembled, the ceiling seemed to drop to inches above their heads, stomach-clutching odours wafted through, fans moved tornadoes of alternatively freezing and burning-hot air, particles of dry ice blasted steaming out of the wall as they approached.

People were packed in the room, stumbling around dazed and looking for a way out. Greg stood blinded and engulfed. Cathy leant against him gasping.

'Crazy,' he said to himself. 'Great!'

'Out, get me out!' she shouted, and he saw she was serious.

He moved to the wall and touched it; it started pulsating under his hand. A sharp electric shock jabbed his wrist. The floor sank soft and rubbery up to his ankles.

Greg fended off others falling into him and dragged Cathy round the room, through the screeching, booming, hollering noise and the insanely flashing lights, testing the walls till they found a section that gave way. They stumbled out; the sound-proof doors swung shut behind them. Flickering corridor lighting was mild by comparison.

'Who – who would enjoy that?' Cathy gasped.

Greg laughed. 'That's the ultimate. Aggression chamber. Any action you make, especially if you try to get out of the room, makes it throw something at you in return. With that many people in there triggering it, it almost goes out of control. Overwhelming. Fantastic.'

'I used to think city rush hours were hard to take, but that was ten times, a hundred times . . . You're enjoying this, aren't you, Greg?'

He smiled at her. 'I am. You're not.'

'I'm afraid I'm not.'

'Then let's bypass the rest. Here, this way.' He'd seen a route marker to the love garden; he'd heard about it but never tried it. She couldn't mind that.

She stopped outside the entry doors. 'No more mind grinding, Greg.'

He kissed her gently. 'Nothing like that.'

Inside it was dark and quiet and spacious. High above, in an artificial sky of stars, was a replica of the full moon shedding just enough light to see by. The floor was landscaped into hillocks and hollows planted with plastic grass, stretching away into the semi-darkness, an imitation of open countryside.

Greg remembered public protests when the love garden was first opened in the pleasure palace. But it hadn't taken long for people to see sense; couples on a rainy day needed somewhere to go to feel alone. Overpopulation meant a quarter of city families shared a single room. Young people had to have somewhere for their love making.

Greg took Cathy's hand and they walked round the edge of the grassed area. It was crowded with couples lying in every hollow. Girls with tangled clothes, men and women moving together, some sleeping, some clutched one above the other, some resting quietly. What had first sounded like gentle artificial wind noise turned out to be continual heavy breathing from all around, a steady sighing, pervading the whole area. And fake summer meadow scent couldn't disguise the tang of sweat and disinfectant.

'It stinks,' Cathy whispered. 'It really stinks.'

'Probably better when you're lying down. The landscaping is to make you feel private, almost like outdoors, except more civilized. God, you know what it's like in an outdoor meadow. Insects, cold wind, damp grass that makes you itch, the ground's hard, it's awful.'

'But . . .'

Nearby a woman stood up straightening her dress. A man followed holding up his trousers with one hand. Greg took Cathy's arm. 'Shall we? Find out how the masses live.'

'Couldn't we . . .'

He took her hand. 'Raining outside, remember? And this is more comfortable than in any car.'

He led her across and sat her down beside him on the rubbery ground. The plastic grass was limp and slimy under her legs. The ground sagged like a soft foam bed. Greg lay beside her holding her to him. 'See what I mean? All you can see is the sky. Like being alone together, Cathy.'

He kissed her pretending not to hear the couple behind him coming to a climax in their love making. She responded stiffly. The ground was heated so that every patch felt as if someone had just been lying there. Her skin prickled. She was rigid with distaste. But then she realized Greg was getting excited, kissing her harder, touching her breasts. She couldn't stop him, not after yesterday; he wanted her now. *Why* she thought *do I always end up making sacrifices to keep the man happy*?

She cut off her thoughts and tried to concentrate more on Greg, his mouth, his hands, his body pressing and moving against hers. He was breathing faster and undoing her dress, touching her bare skin, fondling the swell ings of her breasts.

Greg wanted her badly and having to try and excite her was making him tense and frustrated. The need was urgent as if it might go away if he didn't have her at once. He kissed her hard not really interested in what he was doing or what she was feeling. He pulled her panties down and touched her, trying to pretend she was moist and ready when he knew she was dry and frigid. He'd thought of the love garden as a joke but now he knew it was what he needed, strangely comforting. But no time for thought, now.

She tried to stifle her cry when he entered her. He pushed hard, insensitive, impatient. She hung on to him and her fingernails scratched his shoulders; he thrust her arms down angrily out of the way.

Within moments he realized it was building up and he came quickly, suddenly, almost before he was ready for it. He flopped down on her breathing hard.

He kissed her. 'It was good. I needed it,' he gasped.

'I'm glad,' she said softly.

'You didn't come, did you?'

She smiled thinly. 'I didn't have much chance.'

'Yes. Yes, it was too quick, I'm sorry.'

She kissed him lightly and groped for her underclothes. 'Forget it. Shall we go?'

'You don't want to stay? If you wait a few minutes we could, again . . . it would be better.'

'Somewhere else, Greg. Not here. Take me away. Please. Anywhere.' She was keeping her voice soft, level, holding all emotion back.

They dressed and stood up, picking their way across to the exit. Greg glanced back and saw another couple who'd waited shadowy in the darkness were straight away claiming the spot where he'd made it with Cathy. It didn't seem to mean anything. Nothing told him, physically, that he'd just had sex with her. There was only a brief, vague memory, fast fading in his mind.

Slum Tony

Greg drove away from the pleasure palace with Cathy sitting huddled in her coat muffling her like a barrier to all communication.

'You don't mind what we do, where we go?' he said for the second time.

She shook her head.

'Feel hungry?'

'A bit.'

'Then let's try the café we went to two nights back. In the slum zone. You liked it there.'

She smiled palely. 'Fine.'

Greg drove fast but controlled and with precision, weaving out through the inner suburbs toward the slum zone. Gradually Cathy began to recover herself, relaxed by the hum of the car engine, the rhythm of the windscreen wipers.

When she next looked out they were in a slum street, broken-down, peeling buildings in endless dull lines, drab in the rain. Children ran just out of sight; faces peered half-seen from dirty windows; wild-eyed dogs in packs rooted at random through dustbins and garbage piles. When it was cold and wet in the slums it felt as if it would stay cold and wet for ever.

'It fascinates me you started here,' Cathy said. 'I keep trying to imagine what it's like in those houses, how it feels to live there.'

'If you like,' Greg said slowly, 'I could show you – show you where I used to live. It's not far.'

She turned and smiled, intrigued. 'Why not?'

He suddenly wanted her to see the old place and accelerated down the street. It would be a connection, between then and now.

'Most of my friends moved out of the house when I did; we handed it over to a slummer called Tony, he moved a lot of beats in. I know some of them.'

He parked outside a three-storey terrace house as drab and grey as the rest in the street. Crumbling ornamental masonry, bottle glass strewn over steps up to the front door, which hung on one hinge, lock smashed. The ground-floor bay window was boarded up. Iron railings outside were rusty and bent.

'I want to see inside,' Cathy said.

'It's filthy, and the smell . . .'

She shrugged. 'We can always walk out.'

They locked the car and walked up the steps and through the narrow hallway to a flight of broken-down stairs at the back. The walls were in cream paint turned yellow, paper was peeling off the ceiling, a smashed light bulb hung from a rotted flex. The place stank of damp plaster, damp wood, old linoleum, unwashed flesh. Above it all was the sharp-sweet tang of marijuana smoke.

Greg led Cathy up the stairs past a dirty window half covered by tattered curtaining so faded the pattern on it was almost invisible. 'The beats sleep downstairs, live on the first floor,' Greg explained. He opened the door into the front room. Dim light filtered through cracked, dusty windows overlooking the street. A crowd of ragged men and girls were slumped in chairs and on beds round the edges of the room. Hunched over a centre table was a thin, long-haired man in an incongruously patched, ragged businessman's suit. He glanced up.

'It's Greg, isn't it? Yeah, Greg, great to see you.'

Greg nodded in greeting. He glanced round the room. All the beats were looking at him and Cathy. Their faces were blank.

'Is Tony in?'

The one in the business suit gestured at the ceiling. 'Upstairs. We just scored, Greg, so I got to slice the shit but I'll see you later.' He turned back to the table, littered with cigarette papers, tobacco, a couple of broken razor blades and a lump of hash.

Greg turned and walked out of the room. The beats watched him go.

He led Cathy up to the top floor. On the half landing a phone coin box had been torn away from the wall and smashed open. The telephone receiver hung dead at the end of its frayed cord. Cobwebs had formed between it and the wall.

A partition walled off the top of the stairs. Greg knocked on a door set in one side of it. The panels were split and wood over the mortice lock had been roughly hacked away.

There was the sound of bolts being drawn back. A girl of sixteen in a grimy white shirt hanging outside knee-length jeans opened the door. She had bare feet. Her legs, arms, and face were dirty white and thin.

'Tony here?' asked Greg. The girl turned wordlessly and walked inside. A door opened and shut. They waited. A minute later Tony appeared.

He was tall and wiry, muscular and tanned. He looked twenty but could have been much older. His expression was cool, measured but intense, startling pinpoint pupils set in blue, unblinking eyes. His hair was cut close to his skull.

He paused before speaking, as if weighing them up. 'Been wondering when you'd turn up here,' he said slowly. Muscles in his forearm moved under the skin as he grasped Greg's hand briefly. He glanced at Cathy, taking in her face and figure, then looked away from her. 'Come inside.'

She followed him in, with Greg coming behind.

'Mouse,' called Tony, not looking round. The girl appeared beside him. 'Clear that mess in the back while I'm talking to my friends here.' She hurried into the back room. Tony led them through to the front.

The floor was covered in the centre by a worn, faded carpet thick with ingrained dirt. Burnt matches, cigarette ends, old magazines and dirty clothes were strewn around littering the old linoleum at the edges of the room. The walls were damp and paper was peeling off under the front windows. There was the heavy smell of dry sweat.

Tony flopped down on an unmade bed and put his feet up. Greg sat on some clothes piled on a chair. Cathy walked to the window and looked out; some children were clustered round Greg's shiny sportscar. One was trying to climb on the roof.

'So why're you here?' Tony said.

'Cathy wanted to see the old place. Where I started.' He grinned. 'It hasn't changed, has it?'

Tony looked faintly amused. It was the first time his face had shown anything. 'It hasn't. You have.'

'In some ways,' said Greg. He looked around again at what had once been his own room. He tried to see himself in it, but the images of his memory didn't fit any more. He felt uncomfortable.

Tony had leant over to pick up three cigarette papers from an orange box beside his bed. He licked the edges of the papers and joined them. He cut a lump of hash from a stick lying on the box and roasted the pellet for a moment in silver paper over a match flame. Cathy had turned to watch him but he ignored her, spreading the blackened drug into tobacco lined up along the papers. He rolled the joint carefully, methodically, finally lighting it and inhaling deeply. He looked slowly up at her, then, and held out the joint to her. She hesitated.

'Take it,' he said, watching her intently. 'Don't waste it.'

She took it from him, interested. 'Draw on it deep,' he told her, still watching her with his steady, commanding eyes. 'Hold down the smoke as long as you can.'

Cathy let out her breath and coughed, eyes watering.

'Do you want any?' Tony said sharply, suddenly turning to Greg. Greg shook his head.

Tony smiled. 'Pillhead.' He laughed loudly, briefly, at some private joke and turned away, drawing on the joint again and passing it back to Cathy, casually this time, knowing she wouldn't refuse.

'Don't smoke any more if you don't want to,' said Greg.

Cathy accepted the joint, glancing at him, puzzled. 'It's not exactly opium, is it?'

'How does it feel?' asked Tony, after a while.

She smiled. 'Nice.'

'It's bloody good stuff you're smoking. Not like they got downstairs.'

'Tony deals in it,' Greg said. 'We both did, once, great business set-up . . .'

'Mouse!' Tony shouted. The girl came in immediately. 'Get us some music, while we're turning on here.' She hurried out and Tony looked back at Cathy. She met his eyes and they stared at each other, neither looking away. Greg shifted uncomfortabley, wanting to leave. He couldn't relax. He hated feeling he didn't belong. He couldn't fit.

Mouse brought a battered radio in. 'Tune us some nice music,' said Tony. 'Hell, maybe we get to hear Greg's new sound.' He laughed and Cathy giggled, high on the drug, while Tony started rolling a third joint.

Mouse left the room silently.

Greg glanced at Cathy. 'We ought to leave soon.'

She didn't seem to hear.

'She'll go when she's bloody ready,' Tony said sharply.

Without warning he snatched up a throwing knife from the top of the orange box and in one rippling gesture sent it across the room, smacking deep into the centre of a dart board above Greg's head.

Greg ducked off balance, almost falling off his chair. Tony laughed. 'Go on, you piss off, it don't worry me, kid. Just leave your girl here, right?' His eyes shifted to Cathy. 'She adds class to this dump.'

He lit the new joint and handed it to her.

'Maybe I have had enough,' she said.

'Take it,' Tony said, quiet but firm. 'I'm telling you to.'

She accepted it from him.

'Tony . . .' Greg began.

'Still here, kid? Thought you were leaving.'

'Cut the big tough act. It doesn't impress us.'

Tony laughed as if Greg had made a joke. Cathy smiled. Greg hesitated, then stood up and walked over to her, taking her hand and leading her to the door. 'See you again, Tony,' he said, not looking at the man, annoyed at his nervousness, trying not to show how his hands were trembling.

Tony relaxed on the bed, crossing his legs. 'It'll be all cleaned up here for you, girl, next time you come,' he called as they walked out.

Greg led her down the stairs. Behind them they heard Tony laughing again.

In the street it was still raining. The children ran awav from the car as soon as they saw Greg. He was too preoccupied to look if they'd caused any damage.

'Sorry about Tony,' he said, driving off with Cathy beside him. 'He can be a bastard when he wants to.'

She didn't answer, staring over her shoulder at the house receding behind them. 'You really lived there once?' she said slowly.

'Yes,' he snapped irritably. 'I told you I did.'

She didn't say anything.

'Don't be taken in by that kind of life,' said Greg. 'It's aimless, they don't care about anything, anything in the world.'

'But that's just it,' she said quietly. 'Nothing worries them. That's why they're so self-assured.' She sat relaxed, looking straight ahead, but her eyes weren't focused on anything.

'You're still high on the hash,' Greg told her. 'You aren't seeing things in perspective. When we've had a meal you'll be better.'

'No. Take me home, Greg.'

He hesitated. 'My concert, later on . . . I hoped you'd be able to come . . .'

She sighed. 'I'm sorry. I really don't want to. The pleasure palace was more than enough.'

She seemed a great distance from him, unreachably remote.

He dropped her outside her apartment block and didn't ask to come in. They had said so little during the drive, and he'd wanted to say so much, to talk to her and touch her, make love again. But circumstances had somehow lined up against him. She hardly knew he was there.

'Don't forget to phone me, about the vacation,' he said as she reached for the door handle.

She looked round. 'Yes, of course. All right.'

'We'll have to plan it out together.'

She nodded vaguely, opened the door and got out. He watched her walk up the path and into the apartment building.

He sighed, U-turned and headed back into town, angry and depressed. The vacation was fading like a mirage as he came closer to it. So had Cathy.

He set the car climate control to cold and opened all the air vents. Icy draughts blasted over him.

It helped. By the time he reached the theatre, he could almost face the thought of going on stage.

Breaking the Pattern

In her apartment, Cathy paced aimlessly, lighting cigarettes and forgetting them, half drinking cups of coffee and staring out of the windows for long, dull minutes, seeing nothing. The electric clock hummed. The thick white living-room rug brushed her ankles softly as she walked barefoot, back and forth across it.

Her thoughts nagged in circles. She ought to organize her thinking, but she couldn't face the effort.

In her bedroom she stood looking at the tidy array of dressing-table bottles, brushes and tubes, symmetrically placed cushions on her bed, neatly drawn luxury curtains. Once, each new possession had carried its own excitement.

She frowned, irritated. It was too corny and too easy to

say that luxury hadn't brought lasting happiness. It could have. But not in isolation. How unbearable, now, helping the tired men still coming to her for her kindness. Still worse to be talented at it, at the same time loathing the talent, the way that circumstances always seemed to trap her into relationships where the sympathy and sacrifices were drawn out of her.

She'd slipped into the repetitive pattern of it, she'd told herself it was temporary, that someone would one day appear and alter everything, take her physically and mentally to a new way of life. Greg hadn't done that. He never could, now, though maybe he'd wanted it as much as she had. He had his vitality and his youth but underneath he was as lost and helpless as all of them.

She couldn't go on. She couldn't bear to see Greg join the entourage of her men, coming for his share of her, depending on her. She knew if he came to her like that she'd never be able to refuse him, the compassion would well up in her at the sight of him. That would be unbearable.

Slowly, forcing herself, she took out her suitcases and started packing. She chose only the cheaper clothes and the essentials; it didn't take long.

She left the apartment feeling nothing, noticing her surroundings only with difficulty. So hard, really, to control one's thoughts.

She stepped out of the elevator on the ground floor and walked across the tiled hallway. She reached out for the door catch.

The door swung open before she even touched it. She pulled back her hand, startled like someone woken from a dream. Confronting her was Jamieson, standing hunched forward in pouring rain, dumbly staring at her.

'I'm – I'm sorry, Cathy,' he mumbled, 'but I just had to come and see you. I hope it's not . . .'

She looked away, shutting her eyes.

'I'm leaving,' she said, keeping her voice level.

Jamieson hesitated. 'How – how long for?'

Cathy still wouldn't look at him. 'For good.'

She waited, feeling his eyes still on her. But he said nothing. Finally she glanced at him, and found him standing with mouth open, sad-eyed, rain dribbling down his face and off his chin. 'You can't,' he said. 'You can't.'

She was losing the battle to stifle her emotions. She gripped the suitcase handle hard and tried not to speak. But the more she looked at him standing pathetically in front of her the more it tore her apart.

'Leave me alone, damn you!' she suddenly shouted, pushing past him. 'I'm going to do what I want to do. What *I* want. I'm not going to let you make me feel guilty.'

Jamieson watched, blank-faced, as she hurried away into the evening twilight, rain absorbing her in greyness, until, very soon, she was out of sight.

She Helps Men

It was fifteen minutes after the performance, and Greg was still shaking and sweating, sitting trapped with Owen in the dressing-room while the sub-teens screamed and chanted and hammered and kicked the door, packed in the corridor outside.

'The cops have just got to get here soon,' Greg muttered. The tiny, badly lit room was closing in all the time.

'They *are* here,' said Owen. 'Takes time. They're trying. Don't let it get to you. We're safe so long as we stay inside.'

Greg didn't really hear. He was re-living being on stage when the girls had surged forward in an unstoppable horde, like locusts or ants sensing food, clambering up and chasing him through corridors, over catwalks, up fire escapes until, with Owen, he'd managed to get in the dressing-room and lock the door against them.

'At least it meant I wasn't on stage too long,' he said, talking to hear his own voice.

Owen was peering out of a thin ventilator window,

looking down at the crowds in the street outside. 'Just as well,' he said. 'Your act was bloody terrible.'

Greg cut off an angry comment he'd been going to make and just slumped down in his chair. The pressure was still building up.

'You been holding out on me,' Owen said, turning round and sitting down opposite Greg. 'I fix it, lovely girl, smart vacation just when you need it, and you get hung up on something, you tell me nothing, start lousing up your career. You and me, we don't work that way. You know that.'

Greg sighed. 'Forget the vacation.'

Owen nodded. 'What I thought you'd say. So she won't come, is that it? Jesus, there's other women. Back when you were just starting, I remember . . .'

'That was three months ago, Owen.' Greg's voice was slow and tired but the manager could sense the tight emotion pent up behind the dull words.

'All right,' he said, more gently. 'So now you tell me. What went wrong?'

'I've fouled it all up, with Cathy. That's all.'

Owen stood up, walked across the room and back again. 'Is that so bad?'

'With her, it is. It means something, do you get it?'

Owen shook his head. 'You've gone *soft*, damn it,' he said, his angry voice resounding in the small room. 'For no reason, she gets through to you, in three days you're juvenile love-sick over the woman. I'll tell you, Greg, you try getting tied up with that one and you'll end up just like the rest of them – like that creep you met in the bar. Jamieson. I seen it happen. Christ, I thought you were made of better stuff. I shouldn't have to tell you not to get silly with that kind of girl.'

Greg sat up, feeling his anger rising. 'Say it straight, Owen. Say what you mean, "that kind of girl".'

Their eyes met. Owen stared down at Greg, hands on hips, chewing on his fat lower lip. 'All right, little adolescent kid who ought to know better, I'll really spell it out. She keeps men happy. She's bloody good at it. She's made a fine frying and her men think she's great. A lot of 'em get so they almost worship her. The ones who've got any sense don't let it get that far. They keep it strictly business. Get it?'

Greg was standing now, reaching out, grasping Owen's jacket, shouting 'you're lying, Owen, some scummy trick to get a rise out of me, to get me away from her, You're making me . . .'

'Cut it out!' The big man wrenched Greg's thin wrists away. 'Don't get emotional with me, kid. Face it, all right, so she kind of liked you, more than the rest. You were younger, different, it got you thinking there was something more to her, but shit, if she's not a whore she's the next best . . .'

He broke off as Greg pulled free from Owen's heavy grasp and leapt at the man seeing him as just a vague blur in the tiny closing-in room, grappling for him, striking out at random, fist jarring hard, wet blood splashing, Owen shouting 'Christ's sake don't cut your face, damn you,' trying to get hold of Greg and stop him from marking his perfect features.

Greg couldn't stand it in the room, he suddenly had to get out, the pressure was too great. Before Owen could stop him he'd unlocked the door. He wrenched it open and charged head-down into the tide of girls rushing forward at him.

'Stop! Don't be so damn . . .' Owen's curses were lost as the girls hit the manager in a wave, slamming him back against the wall.

Greg was crawling low, fighting through them, forcing between the soft bodies, punching, elbowing forward, ignoring the scratching, the screaming, the hands and faces. He struggled through the corridor and fought downstairs through the packed bodies to get to his car in the underground park. They swarmed after him, clutching and screaming and trampling one another, clothes tearing, faces flushed, mouths gaping, pink tongues against white teeth, painted fingernails clutching for his skin. He fought them off and got the car door open. They were all around it, under it, on top of it slithering over the roof to him, one got inside with him pressing her face into his, her hand groping between his legs, her mouth on his mouth but all he felt were her teeth and his blood sweet on his tongue. He kneed her in the stomach and kicked out forcing her back. He started the car but couldn't get the door shut, the perpetual screaming was making him dizzy, he just pressed down on the accelerator and forged through them, the screaming turning to shouts of pain as the car bumped through the young bodies, girls clinging to the shiny paintwork. He drove through the exit into the street, police shouting, ambulances everywhere, fire hoses washing fountains of water over the running, shouting girls. He accelerated past a road block, reached across and finally managed to shut the passenger door. There was something thumping on the roof; he glanced up in time to see a girl's face edging forward, craning down through the windscreen at him, her inverted face and obscene mouth sobbing over and over, 'Greg, I want you,' as she clung hopelessly to the roof of the car.

He glanced from her back to the road, only just in time to see a sharp bend. He braked hard and threw the car round the bend, wrenching unnecessarily hard at the steering, realizing too late that he'd taken it too fast, hearing the girl scream as she was flung off, glimpsing her body in the rear view mirror, flying all arms and legs till she hit the ground, tumbling, rolling.

He didn't stop. Grimly, he headed on to Cathy's place.

Alone

She didn't notice much, it wasn't necessary, you could wander through town on reflexes alone, crossing streets, buying coinop meals, muttering apologies when bumping into others on the pavements.

Somewhere she had lost her sense of direction and had

been walking through the rain for a long while, feeling incongruous clutching her suitcase, going nowhere, rejecting each of her friends as she thought of them. There were a hundred places she could stay but they were all part of the pattern of life she'd built up. The pattern she had to break.

She jaywalked across busy streets, intersections, traffic controllers shouting at her, car brakes screeching. Still she didn't know where she wanted to go except away from everything.

Once, it struck her that Greg would be on stage at that moment, at his concert. But she didn't want to think about it.

She realized she'd wandered into the slum zone, and she dimly wondered why. Still, she didn't want to think about that either. Groups of ragged people were standing outside pubs; they turned and looked at her strangely as she walked past with her suitcase.

She decided she must have walked there by chance. It was inconceivable that she'd ever have chosen to go there.

Helpless: No Tomorrow

The turbine roared, headlights flooded the road, other cars flashed by outside his vision. Everything in him added up to a need for her as if she'd taken some vital part of him he was useless without. He sat tense in the driving seat, his shirt torn and his flesh bleeding where the girls had struck with their fingernails. Guiding the car; but not feeling it, not part of anything, watching the traffic like watching a movie, smelling rubber when the wheels span and scrubbed over the road as he pushed the car into corners across intersections over hillcrests faster and harder.

Suddenly he realized he was almost outside Cathy's apartment block. He slowed and double parked, jumping out dripping blood and trailing his ragged shirt as he ran through the rain to the house. There was a crowd on the pavement. He craned his neck to see what they were staring at.

It was Jamieson, stumbling around half naked, his artificial arms gone. His thalidomide hands, joined direct to his shoulders, flapped grotesquely stumpy pink and helpless like stillborn wings. The crowd stood watching horrified but no one wanted to step forward and help the man.

'Doomed!' Jamieson's voice drifted through the still-falling rain. 'Filed! Everything's dying. I'm helpless, we're all helpless. Tomorrow people there is no tomorrow. Cathy's gone, she's gone for good.'

Greg pushed through the crowd and grabbed Jamieson's shoulder, hustling him up the path to the apartment building door. He slapped the man's face.

'Remember me? From the bar last night. Were's Cathy?'

Jamieson tried to focus his eyes but was still incoherent. 'Gone . . . just gone! Through with the luxury life and gone for good.' His face was running with rain and tears.

'Show me,' Greg shouted. 'Show me her apartment. We'll check.'

He hauled Jamieson, still babbling, into the elevator. Getting out on the top floor he found there were only two apartments to choose from.

'This the right door?' He thumped the grey plastic panelling.

Jamieson nodded weakly.

Greg stepped back and kicked violently at the door above the lock. The plastic cracked. He kicked again and it shattered; he barged the door open.

He ran in calling her name but it was all empty, left with the lights burning, curtains not drawn, two burnt-out cigarettes in the ash tray, as if she'd only just gone out and would be straight back.

But in the bedroom, clothes had been thrown carelessly on the bed. The toothbrush was gone from the bathroom and the towels were missing. Greg stood holding his head staring vacantly out of her bedroom window, trying to think. Outside the city lights stretched in a vast panorama;

she could be anywhere among the millions of living, breeding people.

Suddenly he kicked out at the window and the glass gasped outwards from round his foot, shattering and tinkling down to the ground below. But the city was still there after the glass had fallen away.

Cold air swept in. He turned and ran back to Jamieson, crouching whimpering in the corridor outside.

'What did she say? Did she say where she was going?'

'Going for good, she said. Had enough. Of the luxury life.'

Greg grabbed the man and hauled him back into the elevator. He had a sinking suspicion, now. He knew where to look next.

Back in the street he hustled Jamieson through the crowd of people and into the car. He accelerated wildly back down the hill.

Strangely Unresisting

Cathy was still adrift and aimless, still wondering where to go, when she heard them shouting to her from the other end of the echoing rainy street.

She stopped and turned, watching impassively as they came closer. Tony and the crowd from his house were walking back from the pub, drunk and noisy.

'Christ look what's waiting for me here,' Tony said as they reached her. 'Beautiful little Christmas present all for me.'

The rough faces crowded around her, grinning and smelling of raw alcohol and sweat and cigarette smoke. Tony in the middle of them.

She saw and felt him take her arm, but was it really hers, when it felt like someone else's?

He laughed roughly. 'Come back with us, going to be an all-night turn-on, right?' The crowd of shaggy beats shouted and laughed and he took her with him, strangely unresisting, away down the street. The cold streetlight sparkled in the rain in Tony's wiry, ragged hair and his breath rose in white clouds. He looked down at her, into her eyes. She stared up at his shadowy face and he laughed, easy and natural and full of self-assurance, confident and strong, showing his even white teeth.

She wanted suddenly to pull away, he was leading her into something worse than her old life. But her thoughts were frozen and she couldn't break the mood Tony had found her in.

Ahead, his house came into sight.

Tingling with Inaction

He was driving flat out now with Jamieson slumped dumbly in the passenger seat, white faced and wide-eyed in the flashing moving streetlights, staring out at the buildings flicking past, pedestrians jumping out of the way, headlights sweeping, horns blaring at red-light junctions, shopsigns and neons blurred in the night.

'You don't realize what this all means,' Jamieson was mumbling, as if unaware of where he was, the speed they were travelling, what was happening. 'You can only see it on a personal level. But this is the end. See us, see Cathy in relation to the whole population; we're not mere individuals, we are part of everything, we *are* everything. Our lives go to pieces, everyone's lives go to pieces, ten thousand different reasons but all basically the same . . .'

His voice droned on behind the screaming of the turbine and whining of the gears. The car rolled heavily to one side as Greg swung it sliding round a corner at sixty.

'Look at yourself, your life, the pressures that govern it . . .'

'Put your safety harness on,' Greg said sharply as Jamieson fell sideways in his seat and Greg took the car into another curve. 'You might get hurt.'

The man struggled into the straps.

Greg was hardly concentrating, his driving was erratic, it was easy for him to miss the right route. He realized they'd reached the slums but it all looked the same, he was entering the zone from an unusual direction. It was easy to think he knew the road when he didn't. Easy not to see the no-entry signs, he was so dazed. The turbine was roaring so loudly he didn't hear the people shouting for him to stop. It was easy not to see the oncoming car till too late. Glimpse of light. Glaring headlamps. Impact.

The shock happened so fast it was unreal, spinning round in a blur with Jamieson screaming and Greg groaning, flung into his safety harness and the noise of the smash and the metal tearing all in one instant of experience. His sportscar skidded on its side, turning, screaming, rolling, thumping back down on its wheels with windows shattered, cockpit full of glass, one headlight left shining back down the wet black road to where the other car was lying crumpled on its roof.

Greg lay numb for a moment. It was suddenly silent except for rain pattering on the car. Jamieson had stopped screaming. Greg shuddered. The cripple had been thrown out of his safety harness at the shoulders; he had no proper arms to hold him in. His head was a mass of blood and crushed bone.

Greg pulled himself out of the car. More cuts and bruises. It didn't make sense. He felt nothing. Maybe the crash had never happened. He was getting wet in the rain. Two passers-by were trying to rescue the driver of the other car. The man was screaming which meant he was still alive.

Suddenly Greg recognized the street. It clicked and he knew why he was there. He started running, feet slipping on the wet pavement, heading for Tony's place. People shouted for him to stop. But all he had left was his goal. He had to find Cathy.

He was very near now. He knew she must have come there even though he couldn't really admit it. He was shaking so badly it was hard to keep on his feet. Blood kept washing into his eyes where the rain trickled over a cut on his forehead.

And then he turned a corner and it was all laid out in front of him like a stage set. There was Tony's house. There, walking up to it, Tony and the other beats, with Cathy in the middle of them. They hadn't seen Greg.

He watched dumbly, flesh tingling with inaction, rain trickling down his skin, while they got closer and closer to the house. He watched their feet moving them along the pavement. He heard them talking and the sounds echoed across the street and fell at random into his ears.

Then they reached the front steps. Now was the time to run forward, stop her, bring her back, claim her, intervene. Now. Now.

His leg twitched as if wanting to run ahead of its own volition. His throat contracted to form the sound of her name. But he was dumb and paralysed. The people were going into the house, and finally he struggled and managed to utter her name, a hoarse little cry easily drowned by the water running gurgling down the gutter at his feet.

And then, they were gone. Into the house. The door slammed shut. They were inside, and, standing, watching, he felt only impotent.

And when Owen arrived later with ambulances and police cars and lights and newsmen and people shouting, all he could do was slump into their arms like a sleepwalker too exhausted to crawl back home.

Cathy felt lost in the house. She didn't belong. But she didn't belong anywhere, so it made no difference. The beats in the ground-floor room were sitting down on rough, broken furniture under a dim electric light. She saw Tony smile at her and she smiled back weakly; he came over and put his arms round her, and immediately she felt his strength.

'We always turn on here at night,' he said softly, eyes on her. He grinned. 'It's a great scene. Stay here. I'll be right back.' He turned away to the rest of them. 'I feel like *smashing* something,' he shouted, whirling round and grabbing a chair. He raised it high and opened the door of an old wardrobe, smashing the chair down so hard it went right through the panelling, spraying shards of wood amongst the beats. Suddenly they were all shouting and laughing, cutting up the hash they'd brought in with them, dancing to the music from an old cassette player. The sharp-sweet smoke hung under the light in the hot, heavy air, over the heads of figures hunched forward in ragged clothes, turning on, passing the joints, Tony at the centre of them sharing out the hash and seeing everyone had a good time.

Cathy smoked a little of each joint as it was passed to her. She sat numb to the noise and the people, colours flickering at the edge of her vision.

Tony came over to her after a while and pulled her up from her chair. 'Come on, girl. You've had enough.'

He led her up the stairs. Holding on to him, it was as if she could draw power from his body.

His room on the top floor was bleak and depressing in the yellow glow from the old low-power light bulb. He dropped her coat carelessly on the dusty floor and led her to his bed. She followed unresistingly.

But when he held her close to him she smelled the thick, sweat odour of his body and pulled away from him.

'Don't,' he said, capturing her eyes with his. 'Let it happen to you. Come close to me. Feel it sweep over you.'

'I don't . . .'

He smiled, his confident, easy smile. 'You do. Else you wouldn't be here.'

She stood biting her lip, swaying a little, saying nothing.

He lay back on the bed and opened his arms. She went down to him and the smell of his tanned skin closed over her as she lay down and he lay over her, quickly undressing her and then holding her firmly to him. She found herself holding him as he kissed her, pressing herself to him with the taste of him in her mouth. His muscles were strong, rounded, powerful and protecting. He was so natural and calm, as if nothing had ever worried him. His energies, undepleted by city living, were for her. She felt falling backwards losing touch.

When he entered her she shut her eyes and gave way to his strength, feeling one with him yet totally his. And as he went on she found herself opening to him more and he quickened slightly, but still strong and steady, she suddenly cried out and really, really wanted him. The world opened up, the emotion swept over her and she forgot everything, living it, being it, drowning in it.

PART TWO

FIRST PROLOGUE

The longer he was there, the more strongly he felt it. The countryside was different, in a way he'd never expected and still couldn't define. Quietness, openness, monotony, he'd been ready for all that. But . . .

He plunged his fork deep into the hard soil and bore down, dragging up snapping rootlets and uncovering worms squirming blindly in the morning sun.

. . . it was the sense of wrongness . . .

'Julius!'

He turned unhurriedly – he never hurried any more – and waved to Hilary to show he'd heard her. At the other end of the overgrown garden she walked back inside the house.

He yawned, stretched, wiped sweat off his forehead and spiked the fork upright in soil lying as yet unturned. The sun was low, clear and mellow, hot on his bare back and red-brown neck. His head itched under his long, shaggy blonde hair. He moved his stiff arms and started back to the house, the earth crumbly under his bare feet and the tall grass cool between his toes.

The house was wide and old, dust-red brick submerged under voracious creeper that reached up over the roof to clutch at the two chimneys. It was a simple building: three windows upstairs and two downstairs each side of the front door, where a dead rose tree sprawled over the wooden front porch.

The garden stretched two hundred yards, a wilderness of weeds and rotting trees divided by an old gravel drive. At the end of the garden a narrow lane led to a village ten miles away. It was open, flat country and hedges between the endless fields provided the only break in scenic monotony.

The stone floor of the hall chilled Julius's feet as he walked through the house to the kitchen at the back. The house was a confusion of angles, erratic wooden beams that he'd hit his head on when he'd first moved in, walls with mis-shapen bulges and windows in twisted frames that wouldn't shut properly. But the place was as solid as it was old.

She had his breakfast for him in the kitchen. He walked over to where she was standing at the calor gas stove and put his hands round her waist, gently as if unsure why he wanted to. She turned smiling faintly up at him, their eyes met a moment. Hers were plain brown in her plain face, with its gentle but not-quite-pretty lines. *She's cut her hair again,* he thought, his mind drifting. *It's shorter than mine, now.*

"The eggs,' she said, pulling away frowning and turning back to the stove.

He wandered back to the table and sat down, the chair creaking under his weight, his thick beard hiding his expression.

She served the meal, unhurried but efficient and neat, finally sitting down opposite him.

'We need more eggs.'

'Give me a list and I'll drive in this afternoon.'

The scrubbed wood table was square and solid, smooth to the fingers. The walls of the kitchen were whitewashed. The floor was dark, shiny stone slabs cemented together.

He ate methodically, as though the food were tasteless. She watched him for a little while, then looked at her plate as she ate.

'It's just two months, today,' she said.

'Since we came here? Seems longer.'

'No, because if you remember, it was the last week in July . . .'

'What month is this?'

'September, so . . .'

He nodded slowly, looking out of the window.

She sighed. 'The cow's going to calve in just a couple of days, Mr Watson said. He dropped round earlier.'

'He said that last time.'

'This time he's certain. There's things we need Julius, he told me if we didn't have them . . .'

'I'll get them this afternoon if you tell me what they are.'

They fell into silence.

In the other room a wall clock ticked with slow regularity. Birds sang very faintly outside in the garden.

It was always so awfully quiet out in the country.

Julius stared at his food a long moment, his big shoulders hunched forward, chin almost touching his broad chest. His hands tightened slowly on knife and fork and he seemed to cease breathing.

The tension grew and grew inside him and suddenly he stood up, knocking his chair backwards on to the stone flooring. He dropped his knife and fork with a clatter shattering the silence. He strode angrily to the back door and pulled it open banging it against the wall and walking out, abandoning the half-eaten meal on the table.

Alone in the kitchen, Hilary slowly began to cry.

Second Prologue

One evening, soon after they'd moved out of the city, they went out in Julius's big pink station wagon and just drove at random through the country lanes, watching the sunset spread across the cloudless sky. The lanes were narrow, walled in by tall, heavy hedges and hardly wide enough for the Pontiac, but Julius drove hard and wild, throwing the car round the sudden bends, branches and brambles scraping and rattling along the shiny paintwork, the wind rushing past.

Hilary sat close up to him on the wide front seat and they didn't talk at all, he enjoying the feel of driving and the feel of her beside him, she enjoying the passing scenery and Julius, heavy and warm beside her. Sometimes he smiled faintly to himself; they were both so free. The countryside couldn't have been more remote and they were alone in the network of lanes that lay in the open land like a vast intricate carving in the soil.

They climbed a steep hill at full power, the car roaring up the gradient like a big, hungry animal, and then Julius paused at the top and turned down a cart track that took them into the fields. They parked where the country landscape was laid out before them to the haze-soft horizon, no city lights, no sound in the stillness, a scatter of faint yellow pinpoints marking a few isolated farm houses. The sunset faded to a liquid red-black streak along the edge of the deep sky and a thin moon shed a gentlest hint of light to hold the darkness deepest grey.

There in the car with the instrument panel lights glimmering faintly they looked at each other for a moment, feeling strange and different, and when he touched her face and held her to him he was very slow and natural, and she responded more than she had since she couldn't remember when; anyway it was so different she couldn't really make any comparisons.

They climbed into the back of the wagon where there was room to stretch out and move around and she gave herself, pulling up her knees and shutting her eyes, relaxing and feeling him dominate her; it lasted for ever.

Afterwards it was so startling – suddenly realizing the big station wagon was moving under them, swaying from side to side. They wiped circles in the condensation on the windows and peered out. A herd of cows had engulfed the car – it was an island in a sea of cattle jostling round it.

Laughing, Julius pulled his shoes on and leapt out wearing only underpants. He started trying to clear a space through the cows so Hilary could reverse the car back to the lane. But they were obstinate and seemed deliberately obstructive and Hilary laughed so much at his efforts she stalled the car. When he came back in a temper to start it again for her, they looked at one another and forgot about the cows and made love once more in the back. And it was just as good as the first time.

But when it was all over, they found the cows had wandered off, there were thick clouds gathering over the moon, the night seemed empty and colder. Both of them tried not to say anything for fear of spoiling the mood, but it seemed to dissipate of its own accord, and by the time they got back to the house the emotional force had gone, it was very dead between them and they just wanted to get into bed and back into themselves.

The whole of the next day it was cloudy, and it rained.

The Memory

Julius was out walking, on the day they found him. He was carrying the shotgun he'd bought in the village the week before – the twelve bore that still bruised his shoulder every time he tried to use it. Two dead pigeons were tied by their legs to his belt, hanging heads down, eyes shut, swinging and flapping against his trousers as he walked. He was thinking he ought to get a dog, he needed a retriever now that his aim was improving. Though, really, it was hard to justify his shooting at all; there was so much to do at the house, and they had enough money to go on buying meat at the village for years to come.

But into his thoughts came the noise of heavy vehicles in the lane, climbing the hill, faster and louder than any of the farmers' tractors. Puzzled, Julius stepped into the space in front of a gate into a field and waited for the vehicles to reach him.

The first one rounded the corner and he watched it blankly as if he couldn't believe it. It was an old fifteen-ton truck, renovated and painted entirely in chrome, roaring up toward him leading a whole convoy of cars. And numbly he recognized them all, a left-behind memory come back revitalized to confront him. Clement was driving the chrome truck. Following came Ashley Armstrong, the sculptor, in his transparent plastic Rolls Royce. And after him, another truck, the party truck, paintwork a perpetually shifting swirl of semi-liquid colour. Behind that, a battered Plymouth rusting from the body skirts up, like a car with cancer; a low orange sports model on six wide wheels; an air-cushion town car; an ex-army scout vehicle; they were all there.

He stood watching, like a detached spectator; it was only when they were almost upon him that Clement, in the leading truck, saw him and stopped. The convoy came to a halt and Clement jumped down from the cab of the truck, his city-style black cape trailing in the dust, his hand extended, crimson shirt showing inside his maroon jacket cuff. He smiled and the tanned skin crinkled round his tinted blue eyes, staring warmly into Julius's.

'Julius. I almost didn't recognize you standing there.'

Julius shook the extended hand. He looked at the entourage. 'I recognized you.'

'But God you've changed, already, sixteen stone instead of eighteen I should imagine, tanned like one of the natives. Can't have had your hair cut since you left the city.'

'What are you doing out here, Clement?'

The man laughed. He was slim and hard-faced, hair cut short in businessman style, and even when standing still he seemed dynamic, fully charged. He rubbed his hands slowly together. 'Just a social call.'

'You mean, you came out here to see me, and Hilary?'

Clement nodded briskly. 'Why else would we be in this godforsaken part of the country? Look, it's great finding you this way, just when I was getting completely lost. You can navigate us from here.'

Julius paused, staring again at the convoy, people craning out of their cars to see what the holdup was, motors rumbling in the country stillness and exhaust rising on the warm summer air.

'What do you want?' he asked.

Clement shrugged elaborately and spread out his hands.

Already Julius had lost the habit of expressive city dynamism; he felt rural and naive in his slow speech and deliberate movements. 'Wanted to see your place out here,' Clement was saying. 'Maybe have a little party like old times. Reunion. To remind you what civilization's like.' He started back to the chrome truck. 'Besides, makes sense to celebrate while we can, with the state of the country as it is.'

Julius followed him to the truck. 'State of the country? I'm afraid I don't really keep up with the news any more.' He climbed up into the cab, and Clement slammed the door, putting the truck into first gear.

'Real recluse, eh? Depopulation, Julius. Economic chaos. That's the state of the country. Or it soon will be.'

Julius shrugged. 'There's always been economic chaos, as long as I can remember.'

Clement glanced at him shrewdly but said nothing; the noise in the old truck was loud enough to make talking an effort in any case. Julius gave route directions, but otherwise they stayed silent till they reached the house.

Friends

They arrived in the drive and Julius saw Hilary open the front door and come out dressed in her white overalls, holding a broom.

He jumped down from the truck and walked over to her across the gravel littered with weeds. 'Visitors, Hilary! Actual visitors, from the city.'

She looked with narrowed eyes at the convoy roaring up to the house, stirring clouds of dust into the air. The wildly dressed artists and sculptors craned out of the cars and trucks, waving, shouting, throwing confetti that dissolved into pink smoke, revving their engines. They got out of the gaudy vehicles, and pantomimed sniffing the country air and baring themselves to the afternoon sun, capering around, all of them eccentrics and unemployed, the last of the real nonconformists, clothes flapping like outrageous flags. They headed over toward Julius, where he stood in the front porch.

Hilary's face was half-way between suspicion and pleasure. 'What do they want?' she murmured. 'Surely when we left the city we made it plain enough . . .'

'Just a visit, maybe a party,' Clement said.

She nodded slowly. 'Just a visit.'

Bemused, Julius, shook outstretched hands as the people crowded round shouting hello. *Can eight weeks seem so long? Can they make such a change? Do I really know these people?* He fitted names to faces: Charlotte Jones the gallery owner; Rosco Rutherford the electric sculptor; Frankie Garvin masked as usual and carrying his poetry machine; Kristine Kate the model who couldn't stand without posing; Abigail Zuleika with her alphabet harp; and more, old friends, all of them old friends.

'So we'll set things up on the back lawn, right?' Clement was saying.

Julius nodded. 'Well, yes, I think that should be – no, on second thoughts, it might disturb the livestock. And the cow. Better have everyone in front here; but watch out for the vegetable beds.'

They all started laughing and after a short moment he joined in. It was so strange.

Clement shouted directions and immediately the artists made like participants in a military exercise. Out of the swirl-painted party truck came barbecue, juke, sound system, spotlights, colourizers, olfactory, disposable dresses, foam cushions, light curtain machine, masquerade masks, drug dispensers . . . they all helped to set it up while Julius and Hilary watched, and Clement walked back to them at the house.

'Would have given you advance warning if I could,' he said. 'But, if you people won't even have an audio phone connection . . . This is the first free time we've had for days.'

'The workshop's doing well, then?'

'As well as we can, before the bad news breaks.' He paused, glancing round at the shambles of the garden, as if seeing it properly for the first time. 'Photo art scene's gone dead since you walked out on it, Julius. There was no one else who could take over.'

Julius shrugged. 'I'd done all I could. I couldn't go on under pressure like that. There's nothing an artist can do when he dries up.'

Clement looked intently at Julius's bearded face. 'Are you working again yet?'

'Of course he is,' Hilary cut in. 'Digging the garden, cutting grass, milking the goat, he's doing more work than he's done for years.'

Clement forced a laugh but he wasn't amused. There was a moment's silence. Julius cleared his throat. 'Well, we can talk later,' he said. 'You came out here for a party, damn it, let's *have* a party. Hilary, see what we can show them in the way of real food – they haven't tasted any for years. Make this a proper reunion.'

He strode out across the overgrown lawn to the people setting up the electric barbecue and they turned to meet him. Hilary stood watching, face full of misgivings. 'You won't make him . . . that is, why *did* you come out here, Clement?'

He smiled, easily and blandly. 'Julius is right. We can leave the talking, until tomorrow.'

Reunion

The evening was fine and warm and as it slowly got dark they started the portable generator and switched on the lights. Multicoloured beams shone brighter than the sunset, sweeping at random over the garden and transforming the angular fruit trees and beds of sprawling weeds piled up against the fence into sinister, tangled, exotic jungle growths. The barbecue spit turned a cut of synthesteak in front of electric charcoal and wafted appetizing smells that mingled with the heady, sensual odours from the olfactory, plugged in with the lights. The juke started playing twelve-tone rock and randomized soul in the garden stillness, rich wild sounds blasting through the open air and up to the sky, and the people moved to and fro with the music, their clothes shimming in the lights, rustling and rippling in the gentle wind.

Julius mingled with them, moving among them, spreading his personality. They all missed him; they didn't understand why he ever left; they wanted him to start work again; the art workshop had been his idea and it wasn't the same without him running it. Hilary stood to one side watching it all, the same scene she'd watched a hundred times in gallery parties, previews, hotels, the people clustering round Julius, who stood tall and heavy over them while they talked and gesticulated, expounding high-pitched, nervy social talk.

'It's the dirt,' Rosco Rutherford was saying. 'Now, sky, okay, yes okay, in town see sky sometimes, maybe once a week. Grass, now, okay, pseudograss in most tomorrow people's living rooms carpeting the floor. Right? Trees. yeah even trees, in the streets to fight the CO_2 problem right but *dirt,* dirt you don't get. Dust maybe, little bit of soot, but dirt . . .' He bent down and took up a handful of earth, holding it out. 'Look at it, man, lying around all over the place . . .'

Julius smiled. He took a pinch of earth from Rutherford's handful and raised it to his mouth. 'Clean dirt,' he said, swallowing it. 'Harmless.'

Rutherford laughed jerkily. A nervous tic worked to one side of his chin. 'You won't get me doing that,' he said, dropping the earth and shaking its residue from his finger He grimaced as he wiped the last traces off on his fluorescent trousers.

'Julius!' cried a voice from behind. 'You *still* haven't said hello to me.'

He turned and Kristine Kate fell against him into his arms, lips parted, eyes half closed. He hesitated, then touched tongues in her ritual greeting while she snaked her body against him a moment before pulling back.

'Hello,' said Julius.

'That forest back down the road,' someone was saying in the background. 'See it? You see it? I suddenly saw it, like, kind of, like a city, a wooden city. I mean, not like it is now, like, how it could be, trees, I mean, straight and tall know what I mean? Like buildings. Think people'd care if I sawed off branches, planed the trunks square, pour down some concrete maybe, make it, like, a living landscape sculpture, see it? Wooden city. How about that

'. . . to replicate Julius's house, have you been *in* it? so unique I figure I could make the moulds cast it in plastic two-thirds scale so people could crawl round inside, you get it? Run off maybe twenty on the caster then smash the moulds . . .'

'So what does he really get out of living here, anyway? For someone who produced nothing but cityscapes . . .'

'Ask him and find out.'

'No, get him to stand up, tell us all maybe. Sure. Speech, Julius! Speech!'

They all turned and started demanding it, and slowly he moved over to the pillbar and climbed on to it, all six feet six of him, and someone plugged in a microphone and killed the music.

He surveyed the crowds, girls in mirror dresses, '50s replicas, wild hair styles; men masked, sheathed, in flared and pointed suits, scarlet-tipped collars brushing their ear lobes. Painted faces. Polaroid pants. Distorting suits. X-ray shirts and swirl-painted ties. And Julius in his farm clothes, his party suits long since thrown away. He felt ridiculous.

'First of all, well, glad you made it out here,' he started. 'Want you to have a good time. Ball out here like it's in town, right? Move around. Kind of feel the space. Get high on it. Like – like it's the biggest pleasure palace love garden you ever saw. All yours and no one else in miles. Tell me *that* isn't a good place to party in.'

He jumped down and they crowded round. He held up his hands. 'Just have a good time,' he said. He looked at the faces turned his way, curious and expectant. He turned and plunged his hand suddenly into the pill dispenser, grabbed a dozen tablets at random and threw them in his mouth. 'Get stoned!' He shouted. The tension was broken. A few people cheered. The music started again and the lights flashed faster and wilder; someone opened up the barbecue and started cutting off hunks of synthesteak. The crowd shifted over there and Julius went with them until for a moment he glimpsed Hilary, standing back in the shadows, away from it all.

He stopped and turned away from the party, walking over to her.

'Why not join it, this once?' he said.

She managed a smile. 'I never have liked your parties, Julius.'

'Hilary, can't you see how this time it's different?'

She shrugged.

'But we're through with it all, now – through with the city and everything. It can't touch us, we can just get the good times out of it now and forget the rest.'

She sighed, looking up at him. 'You haven't really changed at all.'

He watched her turn and walk slowly back into the house. 'Have *you*?' He shouted after her in sudden anger, as she disappeared inside. At the back of his mind he instantly regretted the anger but she wasn't going to wreck his good time, he wouldn't let her and anyway, the pills were taking hold, he could talk it out with her tomorrow if she still felt bad about it. He started back to the party, beginning to feel good, buoyant, like a ballon floating over the long grass. He was getting used to seeing all the people again; it seemed so long since the last time.

He moved among them, brushing against their crisp clothes, girls with young faces and women's eyes, soft but hard underneath, he knew them all, he'd had them all. The good feeling of people pressing round. So isolated in the country. Now some of the old feeling was back again, building him up so he felt he could do anything.

He took hold of Kristine Kate by her waist and turned

her round; she was all smile and eyes and ivory teeth. 'Kristine, you've been hiding from me, damn it I've been looking for you all over the garden.'

She laughed mechanically, holding herself away from him a little, but he caught her and pulled her close to feel her body under the luminous green gown she was wearing pasted to the length of her skin.

'Anyone would think you got lonely out here, Julius.'

'Sure. Though I have the little woodland creatures to keep me company.'

'Just so long as you don't start fancying the sheep, darling.'

'Well, I do make it with an old cow now and then.' Too nasty, that, but Kate would never notice.

'You crude country folk, with your animal magnetism.'

'Kate, let's walk back down memory lane.'

Their eyes met and she hesitated a fraction of a second before letting him walk her away from the party, into the darkness along the gravel drive. Her face looked suddenly old, lit intermittently by the distant party lights, as she said, 'which memory do you fancy, Julius?'

His fingers were tingling. The cool night air was a caress. He was getting higher and higher and nothing could stop him.

'That time . . . Feb fourteenth, remember?'

'That *was* a social one, wasn't it.'

They sat down together on the ground in the darkness and he felt her expert fingers working to unbutton his clothes.

'Darling, your garments are so quaint.'

'You mean practical.'

'Sure, they come off easy, but . . .'

No more talking then. Re-learning the girl's plastic-surgery body, heavy breasts like artillery shells, indented waist, thighs smooth as science could make them. Daintily she took out her dentures and started kissing down his body, arousing him till he was ready to take her, and it was all very accomplished, slick and smooth with not the slightest clumsiness, she remembering it just like they'd done it six months before on Valentine's Day. And she made it even better, even longer, so when they both came together it was very, very good.

It left him suddenly clear headed. He was still uncoordinated, as if his body were severed from his brain. He could hardly stand. But he felt cool and detached, looking down at the girl with a strange *so-what* feeling, feeling no stimulus from seeing her naked in the shadows, she was so unreal.

'Again darling.'

He shook his head. 'No.'

'You won't see me again for a terrible long time. Wasn't it good?'

'Even more expert than usual.'

She gave a little sigh, sitting up and zipping her clothes on. They glowed green in the darkness.

He just sat there, wondering where it had all gone. It was always a comedown, always had been, but not like this. He reached out and touched one of her breasts before she covered it. She smiled at him. He looked into her empty face.

'Let's get back to the party,' she said. 'We've been out here half an hour.'

He struggled up. 'All right.' He put his arm round her. 'Thanks, Kate.'

She looked up at him, surprised. 'You've never said that before.'

He shrugged. 'Must be the pills in me, I guess.'

Cowboy

Something had happened, back at the party. The juke was still playing loud, and all the lights were on, but most of the people had disappeared.

Julius saw someone dancing with himself on a private high. He caught his arm and turned him round, away from the music for a moment.

'Were'd they go?'

The man's eyes focused slowly on Julius's face. He gestured vaguely at the house. 'Somewhere.'

Julius left him and started round to the back garden with Kristine Kate still following. Further from the music, he could hear some shouting and laughing, sudden screams and people scuffling in the mud of the back yard.

He frowned and hurried nearer. It was very dark in the shadow of the house and he could hardly see the faint silhouettes moving to and fro.

'Cowboy!' someone yelled. 'Shit, I'm the world's last living cowboy!'

Cheers and yells.

There were sheds behind the house, a pigsty, a couple of places for the goats and the cow in its own stall. A shadow-figure blundered out from the yard and walked straight into Julius, bumping off him and staggering away into the night. 'Crazy,' he was shouting. 'Crazy, crazy, crazy.'

'Not so much noise,' called Julius, feeling his way forward. 'The animals . . .'

Suddenly he was among them all.

'Get that?' Someone shouted. 'This animal's noisier than I am, man.'

Something large and heavy stumbled close. People all round were laughing and chattering. Julius realized they'd got the cow out of its stall. Someone was on its back, the others were cheering him, he was waving his hat and making like a horse rider while the cow, heavy with its unborn calf, stumbled in the mud and lowed, tossing its head, hitting the fence and searching round and round in the dark.

'All right, off it,' Julius shouted. He groped for the figure. 'Get off it!'

'What's the matter, you want a ride too, man? No, you're too heavy, this horse, it don't feel so good, you'd . . .'

Cursing, Julius grabbed for the figure, but the drugs made him clumsy and he tripped over himself and fell forward, couldn't stop, hit the side of the cow and felt it under his hands for a moment, wavering off balance, then falling under him sending its rider sprawling into the mud. People were yelling, crowding round, the cow lying on its side giving ghastly shouting groans of pain, thrashing and knocking people with its hooves. The party goers panicked, running into each other and tripping over in a tangle of flapping, gaudy clothes. Julius was shouting for them to clear a space. But people on the outside couldn't see what was happening, they were pressing in to get closer. The screams and shouting echoed off the farm house wall.

Suddenly there was light. Hilary opened the upstairs window, holding a torch, shining it down on the melee and screaming, 'Get out, damn you, all of you, out of this yard.'

'Crazy, crazy, crazy.'

'Get off! Off me!'

'I'm dirty! The dirt ...'

'Jesus what a party.'

Julius fought free, scrambled through the mud-soaked drugged-up yelling city people, blundered across and stood under the window where Hilary was still leaning out, shouting at the party goers.

'Got to go get Mr Watson,' Julius called. 'The cow ... I think, it's going to calve. The shock ...'

Hilary looked down at him. Her face was pale and grim. 'Be quick,' she snapped.

Somehow he found his way out of the back yard. He left the confusion behind, Hilary's voice sounding shrill above the rest but no one listening to her. No one cared. No one was sane or sober.

Julius found his way round the farm house, touching the wall now and then for reference rather than support, walking with great effort, as if climbing laboriously up a steep hill. He searched among the convoy of vehicles for his own car and bumped from one to the next, bruising his shins and knees till he came to the station wagon by chance, stumbling and falling with a bang on to the shiny paintwork of the hood.

He managed to stand up again. The flashing of the party lights was having a hypnotic effect. He fumbled for his keys and dropped them, searched around and found them again, tried a key in the lock, tried another, started laughing to himself and tried to stuff all the keys in the lock at once, told himself to get a grip on things, found the right key at last and got it in, pulled the car door open and fell inside, hitting his head as he slumped down on the seat.

He groaned. He lay on the seat trying to remember where he'd got to go and what he'd got to do. It was only ten minutes to Watson's farm, it should be easy enough.

Maybe he should rest first. He realized he was lying stretched across the front seat. His body felt too massive for him to move unaided. Maybe they should hire a powerful crane to erect him in the driving position. His muscles were dead. Everything was throbbing. He grabbed the steering and started inching himself upright, half made it, then his fingers slipped and he slumped back. Before he knew it, the darkness became complete, and he lost consciousness.

No Communication

When he woke up, it was a beautiful morning.

The first thing he did was groan. The pills had left him feeling weak and sick. Then he started remembering and reconstructing the previous night. Tentatively, he felt himself for injuries. He ached, there were one or two bruises, but that was all.

He sat up. The sky was pale, clear blue, the sun had just risen. It was six-thirty. He opened the car door and got out, breathing deeply, feeling the air cool inside him like a drink of water, spreading out through his drugged tissues.

Slowly he started walking toward the house.

The garden was a shambles. The party equipment had all been knocked over and smashed. Shards of glass and plastic were scattered in the trampled glass. The juke was on its face, lights still glowing weakly in the sun. The pill bar was overturned and multicoloured capsules were strewn like confetti. City people were stretched out everywhere on the ground, asleep, half naked, the wild garish clothes torn and muddy, hair dishevelled, faces smeared and filthy.

It was worse in the back yard. The cowshed roof had caved in – because of people dancing on it? The goats had been turned loose and were gone. Two dead chickens were embedded in the mud. And the cow was still lying in one corner of the yard, dead, spattered with slime and its own blood where it had thrashed around on the ground. Its foetus was half born, lying a third exposed between the animal's hind quarters.

Julius felt sick. He stood looking at the mess and sighed, walking to the back door of the house.

There was nothing that couldn't be replaced, and nothing that would be much trouble to repair, but . . .

He walked into the kitchen and stopped, taken aback to see Hilary sitting at the table in her dressing gown, holding a cup of coffee. For a moment he paused in the doorway and they looked at one another, both of them pale and depressed, wondering if there was anything worth saying.

'Come in and sit down,' she said at last. 'There's some coffee for you, if you want it.'

He walked over and pulled a chair out from under the table. 'No thanks. It wouldn't help.' He sighed. 'I passed out last night, before I even got the car started. That's why I never came back with Watson to help.'

She shrugged. 'I went to bed. I told myself they could sort out their own mess or wallow in it, as they pleased. To hell with them. And that included you.'

He smiled abstractedly. 'Fair enough.'

'It's probably as well that you didn't drive the car. If I'd realized you were as drugged as that . . .'

He looked down at the table top. 'It's all so stupid,' he murmured.

She nodded slowly.

The silence in the kitchen settled over him, but he didn't mind it this time. He needed some silence. They sat for a long while, saying nothing.

Half an hour later, distant sounds of a transistor radio broke into the stillness. It was the morning news bulletin. The noise got louder as the person with the radio came up to the house. Julius looked up and saw Clement open the door. He stopped, looking from Julius to Hilary, snapped off the radio and set it down on the table.

'All right if I sit down?'

Julius nodded. Clement relaxed on a chair and yawned, covering his mouth politely. He was dressed immaculately in clean clothes. His face was pink and clean. He looked brisk, bright, abrasive.

'I'll pay for last night's damage, naturally,' he said. 'Including labour charges for repairs, of course. New livestock, anything else.' He smiled. 'I'm sure you understand, when you have a party, these things can happen.'

'Indeed they can,' murmured Hilary.

'I hope there's no hard feelings. People had a good time, we were all glad to see you again . . .'

'What's on your mind?' Julius interrupted.

Clement paused. 'You and I did agree to have a little talk together,' he said. He looked at his wrist watch. 'We'll have to leave very soon. So the time to talk is now.'

He paused again; Julius and Hilary sat watching him, waiting.

'It had been a couple of months, and no one had heard from you,' Clement went on, looking at his fingernails. 'We were all beginning to wonder . . . See, you're an artist, not a farmer, Julius. You need mental stimulation and you need self expression. The input and the output. You're isolated out here, I've been feeling you might have decided by now, that you made a mistake leaving town like you did. One of the reasons I came out here was that I thought you might be ready to come back.' He glanced up quickly, but kept talking: 'Or, maybe, you've been trying not to think about it. Maybe you can't bear the thought of not having made a success of it, out here. Are you afraid of admitting defeat? Wouldn't you call that narrow-minded?'

'You just want him back in town, making money. You want your thirty-three per cent, like always.' Hilary sighed. 'I knew it, as soon as I saw you driving up to the house yesterday.'

'Maybe you don't realize how much Julius is worth, now,' Clement persisted. 'Values have tripled, since he left the scene. Sure, I know, you've got a good bank balance. But it'd be virtually money for nothing. If you came back to town, perhaps just for only two weeks, it'd be an easy hundred thousand for a couple of city-scapes. They wouldn't have to be good ones, either. You could turn out any old shit, with your reputation behind it.'

'He's not going back,' said Hilary, face firm and grim.

'Then let me get the art materials flown out to you here.'

'You still don't see it,' Julius said quietly. 'I've dried up. Completely. To produce something mediocre is as impossible as producing something good.'

Clement frowned, massaging his face. 'I can't help thinking, it's so dead out here away from town. Anyone'd get depressed. Didn't you feel, last night, the party and the people, the old atmosphere, didn't it put a bit of life in you?'

'Sure. In a way.'

'And it hasn't been a complete success, has it, living alone out here?'

Julius sighed. 'It hasn't. But . . .'

'Then listen, because there won't be another chance after this one. You haven't been keeping up with the news. All right, I'll bring you up-to-date. The government's been covering up all it can for the last six months – maybe for even the last couple of years – but it's leaking out now. It had to, in the end. The birth rate has dropped, to almost nothing, and it's scared the shit out of everyone. Friends of mine, in government, say the talk now is of depopulation, depression, a crash. It's just a whisper now, but growing.'

'I don't get it,' said Julius. 'What effect does the birth rate have . . .'

'Look, the whole economy's based on growth, consumerism. A month-old baby's as much a consumer as you are – food, clothes, space, light, heat – a thousand industries are directly dependent. Ten thousand more depend on them in some way, in turn – retailers, suppliers, and so on. All the industries employ men who spend their wages on products of other industries. You see it now? Sure, a birth rate drop takes time to affect the balance, and government spending can be used in the short term to make up the deficit. But no one knows how long the drop has been covered up. Two years? The crunch is nearer than most people realize. Things can only be kept going for so long, before . . .'

'All they need to do is withdraw contraception methods,' said Hilary.

'You think no one's thought of that? It's not the answer. Something's happened, no one knows what. Psychological, biological . . . all I know is, women aren't having children. And the economy's showing the strain.'

'What are you leading up to?'

'All I'm saying is, there isn't much time. When deflation really sets in, the luxury markets suffer first and most. The art market, for instance, now do you see why it's urgent? We can sell your work for a fortune. In a month or less, it'll be worthless. See sense, Julius, turn out some crap, *anything*, we'll clean up for ourselves and go our separate ways. You'll do a week's work and then be free to go anywhere, town, country, whatever you want.'

Julius looked thoughtfully at the trees outside the kitchen window. 'Even if you're right,' he said slowly, 'it doesn't seem to matter; even if I could work again, I wouldn't want to. I'm not interested in the money. We have enough. And I can't go back to the old rituals. Life out here isn't perfect, but maybe no perfect solution exists. The city would certainly be worse. Hilary dragged me out here and she was right, it was killing me, all the different pressures. City people think they have energy, vitality, but it's all nervous, it's not something you can go on giving out forever. It drains people of all they've got, and I'm not going back to it.'

Clement paused a moment, hands flat on the table top, then shook his head in resignation and pushed back his chair. 'All right,' he said. 'Then that's it. I guess our old, formal contract has terminated, Julius. I thought I could come out here and persuade you, but . . . I'll have to go back straight away, now, there's so little time. The news this morning . . . I'm expecting petrol rationing, any day now. The next move'll be to get everyone into cities, centralize everything to cut down distribution costs . . .'

'That'll only make things worse,' Hilary broke in.

Clement shrugged. 'It's what's going to happen, right or wrong. If you've got any sense you'll stockpile all the petrol you can get. Keep it locked up, or better still, hidden. I mean it. Take all your money out of the bank, sell your shares and turn everything into capital goods – food stocks, guns, clothing, a power generator. It'll all be worth ten times as much, a year from now, when money'll be worth nothing.' He paused, opening the back door, and looked up directly at Julius. 'It's a pity this didn't work out. See you again, one day. It was a good partnership while it lasted.'

And with that he was gone, striding quickly out of the house into the sun, shoulders hunched forward, forehead tensed into a frown, his hands thrust hard into his pockets. Behind him, in the kitchen, Julius and Hilary sat quiet and relaxed, untouched, undisturbed.

'Sure you won't have any coffee?' she asked him.

Julius yawned, looking thoughtful. He shook his head.

'I'll make some more, just for myself, then.' She stood up, walked to the stove and put the kettle on.

'Do you think there's anything in what he said?' Julius asked her.

Hilary shrugged. 'It's a scare. You know how it happens,

businessmen always panic first. People will start having children again next year.'

Julius stayed sitting at the table, still looking out of the window.

Some time later, he got up from the table, rummaged in a drawer in the kitchen dresser, and sat down again with pencil and paper. He started making a list. At the top he put, petrol cans. Below that, he started listing food.

'While we were in the city,' he said, still writing, 'you know, we hardly ever made love properly, let alone thinking about children.'

First Postscript

That afternoon, he and Hilary started clearing up the mess in the garden. Clement had left it all: the juke, the lights, the overturned pill bar, the barbecue. He'd woken the drugged artists and herded them impatiently into their trucks and cars. Within minutes the convoy of vehicles had moved out along the drive and disappeared down the road, the rumble of their engines fading into nothing, leaving only the still peace of the garden.

It had turned into a hot day and Julius found himself more irritable the hotter he got, working in the sun on the cowshed roof, fighting flies away from his sweat-filmed skin and making more and more mistakes laying the new asphalt sheeting where the old had been broken by the party-goers. When he realized the last piece of covering he'd cut was a foot too short he just threw it down into the yard. 'What's the point,' he said. 'Tell me, what *is* the point.'

Hilary sighed, standing up and massaging her back. Her arms ached from sweeping up the mess. 'I know,' she said, sighing. 'I know.'

'Damn Clement.'

'Because he made you admit it wasn't working out here? But you said . . .'

'I know what I said. But he sowed the seeds of discontent even if he didn't realize it.'

'You don't want to go back to town. Say you don't.'

'I don't, but it doesn't make this place any more attractive.'

'You're just in a bad mood. You've always said this was such a great idea.'

'Sure, it was such a contrast at first. It seemed perfect.'

Hilary sighed. 'I don't know what to do about replacing the animals. It's such a job feeding them all, looking after them. Damn it, I'm *glad* that cow died . . .'

'And winter's coming. That'll mean more work. It's been easy so far, by comparison.'

She looked up at him. 'All right, Julius, what's your answer? You said yourself, there probably isn't an answer. What do you really want to do?'

He swung down from the half-finished cowshed roof and started brushing dirt off his clothes and hands. 'I've had enough, Hilary. Let's move out.'

'For God's sake, if you can't be reasonable about it . . .

'I'm reasonable. It's pretty here, it's open and free. But damn it, so what. Sometimes I just want some *noise*, you know? Or at least something round me. The buildings. I miss the buildings most of all. And you – sometimes I can see you're unhappy, the way you stare out of the window without saying anything.'

'But we can't go back, so what . . .'

'We'll just have to move on. I don't know where. We'll find something, though. There's no sense in seeing only two alternatives when there may be hundreds. This one didn't work. Let's face the fact. Right?'

She stood thinking about it for a moment. At length she smiled sadly, turning to him. 'I guess the house'll still be here for us to come back to, if we need it.'

'Right.'

Second Postscript

They drove through all that evening and through the night, heading north, along the main routes. The wagon was crammed with cans of petrol and a few belongings, the shotgun, a rifle, blankets, primus stove, plastic ground sheets, a tent, piles of tins and food packs, a drum of drinking water.

The further north they drove, the wilder the countryside became, colder and bleaker, the hills rising into mountains that stood gaunt and grey like old fossilized bones protruding through the earth's skin. The roads became rougher and the traffic sparser until, on the fifth day, they drove all morning and saw no one, and felt as if the rest of the world had died behind them. The petrol stations were more primitive and further and further apart, and many were closed, as if to confirm Clement's warnings. Julius wondered what had happened, and speculated a lot, but eight weeks away from the city had dulled his interest in the world and its events. With Hilary, he felt self-sufficient anyway. Nothing really worried them and they couldn't be bothered to stop in the villages they passed through. So they never found out what the news was, or even if there was any.

They drove on and wondered how long the car would run before something went wrong with it. There was a lot of noise coming from the front somewhere and getting louder, like a bearing running dry of oil; but again, it didn't seem to matter, the important thing was to keep moving, to drive on and on into the north and deeper among the mountains.

When the car finally failed them it was their sixth day out, atop a mountain road that hairpinned down into a narrow valley where a lake lay far below in a patch of rough, dark green land scattered with stunted, wiry trees. The engine died and wouldn't re-start. Feeling unsurprised, somehow, Julius switched off the ignition and just let the car coast down the steep road for a full fifteen minutes, all the time looking for a place to pull off the road and stop. But the mountain face was sheer grey rock on one side and it dropped cleanly away on the other. So they coasted on almost to the bottom of the valley, the snow-smeared mountain peaks towering high all round them.

Just when they'd both agreed to sleep in the car and continue on foot the next day, they saw a narrow track leading off the road up to a small cottage set right against the mountainside and built from the same grey stone. Julius turned the car on to the track, finally stopping a few yards from the door of the little cottage.

They went inside. It was empty but dry, obviously not lived in recently. All they could find was a couple of pairs of worn-out socks in the bottom of a roughly made wardrobe in the back room. Hilary moved a lot of their living essentials into the little building, planning to lodge there for a couple of days. They found there was a tap piping water down from a well higher up the mountain, but there was no electricity, not even calor gas, so they cooked on their primus and used oil lamps in the evening, though they usually went to bed soon after sunset, anyway.

During the next few days Julius explored the surrounding countryside. The cottage was only a few hundred feet above the valley floor, and Julius managed to shoot some rabbits, ducks, once a fox, and started fishing in the small lake. Hilary planted vegetables in a square of thin, sparse soil near the cottage. But she and Julius made no pretence of permanence.

It was several weeks before Julius met anyone, and when he did, it was the owner of the cottage and of most of the land in the valley. But he was moving to the city, and was happy to let Julius and Hilary stay in the cottage, now that the tourist trade which had once supported him had died out completely, with the coming of what he called 'the crisis'.

Julius didn't ask the man for news, but a few days later he went for a long walk following the mountain road to a village fifteen miles away, and when he got there he found it deserted, the houses empty and the shops bare of food. Under the counter in one of the shops was a newspaper. It was a single badly-printed sheet, and it was a couple of weeks old. He put it in his pocket and found a few tins of food hidden in one of the empty houses before returning to Hilary and their cottage.

That evening they studied the newspaper trying to make sense of it, but the journalism was hard and slick and referred to a hundred things that had happened in previous weeks, making little sense. The back of the sheet was entirely given over to a list of new government regulations controlling the lives of citizens in so many ways it seemed practically every freedom had been abolished. There were warnings against looting, against 'loners' breaking away from the town centres, against any 'further rioting, incitement to riot, demonstrations and disturbances'.

Julius and Hilary lost interest in the news soon enough since it didn't relate to them in any way. A few weeks later when he wanted to look at the newspaper again he found Hilary had thrown it away long since.

And so they lived on in the cottage, self-sufficient and in equilibrium.

At the end of their first year there, they no longer thought about the passage of time, hardly spoke to each other and lived an abstract existence in complete harmony with the stark landscape. Often they would sit together in the evening, by the rusting shell of the station wagon, and watch the slow sunset spreading colours across the snow-topped mountains, each evening a subtly different sequence from the last, the snow glittering pink and gold, the mountains like skyscrapers of rock silhouetted black against the stars when night closed in. The mountains, walling in the valley, became as much a part of Julius's life as the cottage itself. He felt their presence, whatever he was doing.

No one ever came along the mountain road, and they forgot why. But if they'd had a visitor, and he'd asked them, Julius and Hilary would have probably said, after a bit of thought, that they were contented.

PART THREE

Centremart – 1

Cement powdered with a bang in front of him and dust settled gently from the small crater left by the bullet. Johnson froze unable at first to assimilate the fact of the gunshot. Then he panicked and started running as two more shots sounded from behind him, echoing round the deserted centremart.

His civic suit flapped tripping him as he ran gasping and trembling up ramps and round pillars, through tunnels and into the shopping complex, under signs, through empty supermarts, dodging and glancing behind him at half-seen pursuers, pausing and trying to listen above the noise of his breathing, hearing distant voices shouting directions to one another.

He'd never expected them to turn on him, to shoot without warning. From deserter he was transformed into fugitive. Hiding places were on all sides in the maze of walkways and buildings, but nowhere was safe from his pursuers.

Chest aching, muscles limp and dragging, eyes unfocused, he blundered from one empty building to the next, stumbling, colliding with walls, finally tripping and falling head first from an upper level. For one astonished instant he saw the uprushing ground, and then nothing.

Lone Zone

The tiny, white-walled kitchenette was dusty, cold, and damp. Its grey plastic floor drained the warmth from Reid's bare feet. He stood holding his hands over the little heater where breakfast was cooking and wished it were early spring instead of late autumn.

He reached out, rubbed grime off the window and peered down into the shadowy street. Fifteen stories below, the road was a dark strip walled in by the grim faces of the apartment blocks planted either side in neat, close-spaced lines. But above, where the buildings caught the early morning sunlight, their white concrete was transformed into a mosaic of pastel reds and pinks, rectangular patterns of sparkling sunrise colours crowding up into the cold blue sky.

Reid's breath, hanging in front of him in the frigid air, misted the little window and blurred the colour patterns as if by shifting them out of focus. Serious-faced, he traced paths in the condensation with his fingertip, studying how the tiny water droplets united into glittering rivulets refracting the golden light from outside and running down the glass like threads of fire. The city was cold and empty and lifeless; but sometimes it was beautiful.

The smell of cooked food ended his reverie. He turned, found the vakpaks were ready and slit their filmy plastic seals, emptying the food into three plastic bowls. From a cupboard he took spoons, wiping the dust off them with his fingers. Then he carried the bowls into the adjoining room where he, Amanda, and Vincent had spent the night together.

He paused in the doorway. Pale winter sunlight was filtering through the single dust-patterned window, touching Amanda's face where she lay asleep with Vincent, huddled under a single durafelt blanket. Reid looked on her features with a mixture of emotions – tenderness, compassion, detachment. Age was encroaching, small wrinkles were deepening in the weather-tanned skin; she was almost forty now. Yet she retained a passive, undemanding attitude to life and her face reflected this in its serenity. That kind of beauty she would never lose.

The smell of the food awakened her and she rolled over, sitting up in the narrow bed and revealing her browned, compact body. She brushed her long dark hair out of her face and smiled, still sleepy. Vincent slept on undisturbed beside her.

Reid sat down and she kissed him gently on the lips before taking one of the bowls of food from him. They ate the breakfast paste without speaking, enjoying the relaxed silence of early morning.

The little bedroom was sparsely furnished. Two narrow beds, a built-in cupboard and a single plastic chair occupied most of the floorspace. Everything was dust-filmed and the room smelled dead, as if all life had long since disappeared. The other apartments, in that block and all other blocks in linear city seven, were the same – sealed containers of slow time, empty and bare as monastic cells, depopulated, in one of the lone zones.

Reid, Amanda, and Vincent were wanderers, stopping overnight in the cramped little rooms, voices ringing off the white, pre-cast walls and ceilings, feet stirring the carpet of dust. Soon they would move on and abandon the apartment as one would a drab hotel suite.

Amanda finished her food and shook Vincent awake; he opened his eyes and smiled at her, pulling her down to him for a moment, firm but gentle. He held her to him cushioned by her breasts, and kissed her unhurriedly. They broke apart after a moment and he ran a finger down her smooth bare back as she turned and swung her legs over the side of the bed. At the other end of the room, Reid had begun dressing.

Vincent was tall, well built, firm-muscled and firm-featured. His wiry blonde hair fell in shallow waves to his shoulders; his tanned face showed a calm, experienced competence in living. Each movement was judged. Reid and Amanda followed him as a leader, though at the same time sharing a strong, subtle form of equality.

While Amanda brushed her hair and Vincent finished his meal, Reid pulled on a pair of plastic shoes and walked to the window, looking out over the deserted concrete landscape softened in early morning haze. In the distance there was a flicker of movement; the morning train on its elevated monorail winding between the buildings. Sunlight flashed on its bright steel cars.

The monorail linked the few remaining civic centres scattered over the country, relics of centralized urban life, where small civic populations were slowly losing their battle to retain traditional society in the face of inevitable depopulation.

Two trains a day, morning and evening, were the last signs of organized life. They never stopped in the lone zones, the linear cities where scattered groups of loners like Reid, Vincent, and Amanda wandered in isolation among the empty buildings. Dedicated to conservatism, the civics despised loner life as being devoid of purpose or principles.

Reid's attention turned to a complex of department stores and supermarts several blocks distant.

'We could visit the centremart today,' he said. He turned round. 'All right?'

Vincent nodded. 'I wanted to anyway.'

'And after that, back south again? We're at the edge of the zone.'

'I planned on staying here quite a while yet.'

Reid frowned. 'It's been a week already. I feel like something new.'

'Not yet.' Vincent smiled, pleasant but firm. 'There's time enough, Reid. Time for everything.'

Reid was ten years younger than the other two. He turned away.

When they were ready, the loners walked out of the apartment, leaving the door open and the tangled bedclothes and dirty breakfast bowls on the floor behind them.

The apartment building corridor was lined with identical grey doors, each stencilled with its number. The place was cold, dim, smelling of damp decay, but where the loners' feet stirred the dust the plastic floor showed through bright and new, as unmarked as when it had been laid thirty years before. No one had ever lived in the building. After depopulation, no one ever would.

Elevators were unreliable so they took the emergency stairs down to street level. The stairwell was narrow and grim; many steps were ice-covered where water had seeped in through cracks. The ice would stay frozen, the loners knew, for the rest of the long winter.

In the wide street outside the concrete buildings towered precise and regular like vast featureless tombstones marking the graves of the unborn. The dry, cold air shimmered in the faint heat from fingers of sunlight slanting between the massive blocks; their topmost windows caught the sun and shone in a blazing glory of orange and crimson.

The scene was vast and empty, and totally silent.

Walking down the centre of the deserted six-land boulevard, the loners' shadows stretched out in front of them.

'It must have been the last section of the city to be built,' Reid said quietly. 'Some buildings are almost as new.'

'Still it's aged since we were last here,' Vincent said. He gestured at small piles of rubble and loose dirt accumulated at the bottoms of the buildings.

Amanda sighed. 'The older the city gets, the older I feel.'

CENTREMART – 2

They turned a corner. High over the street, great traffic signs hung like vast heraldic banners, emblazoned with Da-glo route directions. And further on, crowding each side of a three-level street interchange, the centremart was a complex of curving ramps linking the shopping levels, walkways bridging the wide street, route indicators to filter the non-existent traffic, arrows designating pedestrian priority zones, electric signposts to eating houses and fallout shelters, public lavatories and play zones. Tall hoardings displaying faded consumer messages fronted the concrete façades of the sprawling buildings.

Dwarfed by them, the loners walked down an underpath and up a ramp past store windows piled with stacks of untouched goods. The entire centremart had been stocked before the zone ever opened to residents, and before the depopulation crisis. In every store the bright-wrapped food and consumer goods lay in piles for the people who had never come, and never would.

They walked on slowly, through strips of sun and shade, sometimes stopping and looking, occasionally speaking to one another. The wide blue sky hung over them like an ice-cold, depthless pool. The pale sun shone weakly, touching the scene with gentle light.

They turned off the main precinct, skirted a curved pedestrian ramp sweeping up across the sky, and found a narrow passage between two buildings. The alley was like the bottom of a crevasse; their footsteps boomed and echoed as they walked along the interleaved steel power-path.

Lying up against a pillar supporting an upper-level ramp was what looked like a bundle of rags. They noticed it but paid little attention until, when they were almost upon it, Reid, ahead of the other two, stopped and looked closer. He turned, beckoning them to him.

From under the ragged, rumpled clothing a hand was sticking out, white on the ground in the sun, the fingers spread slightly, dried blood on the skin where there was a small cut.

The loners paused uncertainly.

To meet anyone was unusual; loner groups seldom encountered one another in the wilderness of empty buildings. To find a man on his own, and injured, was still rarer; loners always kept within their small units.

'Do you think he's dead?' Reid said at last.

'They wouldn't have just abandoned him,' said Amanda.

Vincent grunted and bent over the man, pulling the coat off him and turning him on his back.

'A civic,' he said quietly.

They stared down at the man's pale, lined face, balding head and strangely tailored clothes on his thin body.

Reid looked up uneasily. 'He's got no business here,' he said.

'Maybe dumped, from a train,' Vincent said. 'But they usually bury their dead.'

Amanda shivered. 'Today felt like just any day. This is unreal.'

'But look, he isn't dead,' said Reid. The civic's head was cut and bruised but he was still breathing, slowly and lightly.

'There must be a reason for his being here,' said Vincent.

Reid looked worried. 'Leave him. Let's leave him. Only means trouble.'

Vincent looked amused. 'You wanted to see something new. Here it is.'

'But he just has to mean trouble. Hasn't been a civic in a lone zone for ten, fifteen years. He didn't get here by accident. Those bastards don't let anything happen by accident.'

'Still, aren't you interested, Reid? We all hate his guts on principle, but he could be important. We ought to find out.'

'So strange to find him this way,' Amanda said softly, 'as if we were *meant* to.'

At that moment the civic's eyes opened. He blinked, coughing, wincing, and turned his thin, pale face from side to side, staring up at them. 'Loners,' he whispered to himself.

Amanda knelt down beside him. 'Do you want help?'

Something passed through the civic's eyes. 'Yes – yes, but I must warn you . . .' He managed to stand up. 'Johnson,' he gasped. 'My name is Johnson.'

They took him to the nearest department store, Amanda helping him walk. He shivered constantly, breathing hard, limping. Vincent led the way and Reid followed resentfully at the rear. No one spoke.

The store was fifteen storeys high, standing ugly and squat among the other buildings, served by clusters of curving ramps and roadways. In the ground-floor supermart lit dimly by a few remaining glow panels they laid Johnson on a pile of empty cartons in one corner.

'Is there edible food? Something to drink?' he gasped, still shaking. Vincent and Reid stayed by him while Amanda toured the shadowy aisles selecting packaged food from the red plastic shelving.

Then they gathered round the civic, opening vakpaks with their teeth and offering him food and capsuled drinks. He ate sparingly, nervous and clumsy, his pinched white face turning from one loner to the next, searching for a clue in their impassive expressions. They were studying him, finding him hard to believe in; he had little reality in a landscape that was theirs.

'The first thing is why you're here,' said Vincent.

'I fell,' Johnson answered, voice weak and accent archaic, learnt from decades-old civic language tapes. 'I hit my head, knocked myself out . . .'

'We know that.' They sat waiting, watchful and demanding.

'I'm from Cenlon.' He smiled uneasily. 'I'm . . . well, I'm running from the authorities. Took the evening train last night and jumped when it slowed for a curve. I slept in an empty store . . .'

Vincent shook his head. 'I don't think I can believe that.'

'What do you mean?'

'He means there's no reason why a civic should ever run

here,' Reid said. 'Your kind can only live one way. It's not our way. You know that.'

Johnson sighed. 'You don't understand, it isn't so simple. Things have tightened up in all the civic centres. They need a stable society to support the organized population research – still hoping to reverse the birth rate trend. But things have gone on getting worse. It's much more difficult, the sex ratio has reached three to one and there's still enforced monogamy.'

Vincent frowned. 'Three men to every woman?'

Johnson nodded, still weak from the escape from his pursuers. 'The birth rate's low enough, but still falling, and what babies are born are male. It makes no sense now to toughen up the laws, pile on further restrictions and preserve the old social structure. I wrote to the city governor, suggested a more liberal line, but the next day a friend of mine in government warned me, my name had been put on the arrest list. I had to run, they can hold you on anything now. Subversion, for instance, is a very vague charge. It carries ten years minimum.'

'For just writing a letter?'

Johnson hesitated, glancing from one loner to the next. 'The laws been strengthened ever since the crisis, and anti-liberal propaganda has worked people up, against any non-conformist, loners most of all. There has to be a group that people can despise. There's no other release. They're so afraid of things fragmenting.'

The loners sat in silence for a moment, Vincent leaning forward intently, Reid sitting further back and showing his hostility, Amanda to one side, face calm and composed.

'What did you mean when you said you had to warn us?' asked Vincent.

'A civic police unit is out searching for me. They found me this morning, it was close, they shot at me but I lost them in the buildings, before I fell. Then . . . well, I hadn't expected to meet loners. I saw you and realized, to the civic police it doesn't matter if they get me or loners like you, so long as they get someone. You and I have a common enemy. We're in equal danger.'

There was another short silence. Vincent started to speak but looked round when Reid stood up abruptly, angry and antagonistic. 'You try to sound like us, and it all comes out very smooth and clever. Convincing. But you're still a civic, nothing can change that. Inbred, skin pale like you've never seen the sun, hair falling out, under-nourished, all kinds of civic diseases – you shouldn't have ever come here. And we shouldn't have picked you up. We should have left you where we found you.'

'I – I don't mean to cause any trouble.'

'Just tell us what you do want. And what you're offering,' Vincent said quietly.

Johnson scratched his balding head. 'I don't understand. I brought you a warning, that you're in danger. I ask nothing, just thought we could stick together for a while, hide out somewhere, something. You could show me how you live out here, teach me how to survive. I'm just like you, an outcast. Lone zones are my only refuge.'

His eyes were wide and innocent, his expression unashamedly appealing.

Vincent laughed suddenly. The sound echoed under the low supermart ceiling. 'All right, you say you're different from the other civics. Maybe you are; how do we know? Why should we trust you? Hasn't been a civic in a lone zone for ten years and the last one was lynched. But I can't help being interested, however much we all despise what you come from. So don't expect anything from us – from our group – and don't interfere. Agree to that and you can stay with us for a while.'

Johnson smiled. 'Thanks.'

Vincent looked non-committal. 'To me you look like you're holding something back. Say what it is and we'll work better together.'

For a moment Johnson wavered, then shook his head. 'I've told you everything.'

'But he can't help but cause trouble,' Reid cut in. 'He'll upset how we live, we can't trust anything he says.'

'We're not so insecure and vulnerable,' said Amanda.

'To me, the way we found him, as if by chance yet as if on purpose – that's reason not to ignore him.'

Reid looked at her, then back at Vincent. He shook his head and said nothing.

'Would the civics who shot at you still be in this area?' asked Vincent.

Johnson looked up. 'Yes, still searching, I expect. But you know the territory, they don't.'

'Better find a lookout point, see if we can spot them, decide on the safest route out of the centremart,' Vincent said to himself.

'The pleasure palace roof is highest,' Reid said.

Vincent nodded. 'We'll try it.'

Static Scene

They took a stairway up into the department store first floor. Footsteps echoed in the yawningly empty expanse of plastic flooring and goods displays. They threaded their way past hoverbeds, cosmetic masks, synthefood, electrostatic cleaners and dream-relax machines. Up escalators jammed stationary and silted with dust; through lifeless automatic doors.

The clothing department was cluttered with displays of rotting tomorrow suits fashionable thirty years ago. Johnson grasped Vincent's shoulder as they were starting up to the next level.

'Could I just . . . just stop and get something to keep me warmer? Civic clothes . . .'

Vincent glanced at the man's thin plastic-weave civic work suit. He shrugged. 'All right. But quickly.'

They put Johnson in front of a foto fitter. Vincent read off measurements and punched buttons. Somewhere a tired, corroded mechanism ground into reluctant motion and a two-piece fibre garment like those worn by the loners ejected into an armour-glass deposit cubicle. Johnson plucked futilely at the door catch.

Vincent laughed. 'You mean you forgot your credit card?' He pushed Johnson aside, stood back and kicked the card-reader mechanism to pieces. The door swung open.

Vincent tugged out the tough, free-fitting clothes and dumped them in the civic's arms. He struggled into them and followed the loners up to the next level.

'Pleasure palace this way through,' said Vincent. They vaulted pay-stiles and followed signs along a corridor and out over a glass pedestrian bridge spanning a concrete chasm that stretched right down to the deserted, black-asphalt road.

Fusion generators had been incorporated in linear city plans to provide power unattended for decades. Thus in the pleasure palace some of the effects still worked; corridors pulsed at intervals with shifting, erratic light that flowed like colour waterfalls. But the sound systems had long since failed; the only noise was the loners' footsteps and breathing as they hurried through.

They took an emergency exit and abruptly were outside the building on an iron fire escape, rusty lattice of metal up over the parapet and on to the pleasure palace roof.

It was cold, isolated, open, and desolate. The rest of the shopping complex stretched out on all sides, a chaos of thrusting, tangled steel and concrete curves and columns, interwoven with monorail tracks and pedestrian pathways. Oblique sunlight camouflaged great areas in shadow, transforming other parts into a confusing light-shade mosaic, patterns, meshing. Further out, surrounding the shopping complex, the tall blocks of the residential zone spread into the distance. And two miles beyond them, further north, lone zone merged into civic centre and older, soot-marked buildings supplanted the stark, perpendicular geometry of bare concrete.

Vincent leaned on the parapet and scanned the vista of buildings. There was nothing to see, no movement, no break in the static scene.

The light suddenly dimmed and they glanced up as a

shadow spread over the city, a high white cloud creeping over the pale sun.

Amanda shivered. 'Snow soon,' she said. 'I can feel it.'

Vincent ignored her. He pointed at a roof on a building two blocks distant, a few storeys lower. 'There. See it?'

Everyone looked. For a moment they saw nothing, but then the sun brightened again and there was a faint, brief flash of reflected light.

Vincent turned to Johnson. 'Someone's watching us.'

They stood in silence, the only sound their breathing, the only movement the rising whisps of exhaled frost-white air.

'Let's get away from here,' Amanda said uneasily. It feels . . . wrong. The city. We'd be safer in a different part.'

Reid wrinkled his nose and scowled. 'We could go across there and face those civics, meet them head on.'

Vincent shook his head. 'It'd be pointless. We're unarmed and we don't know how many of them there are. Amanda's right.'

He turned and started back down the fire escape to the emergency exit into the building. Amanda followed, then Reid. Johnson looked round to see the last loner disappearing out of sight. He hurried after them.

Alone in the Pleasure Palace

It was easy to get left behind, easy to get lost. Reid, Vincent, and Amanda followed the convolutions of the corridors and stairways as easily as tracing a path through a map; they'd explored it all before. Johnson stumbled and tried to keep pace but many passages were unlit, cavern-dark, concrete walls closing in each side and footsteps of the loners receding ahead. His legs were tired and his lungs ached with the cold and the effort of breathing; and suddenly, he was on his own.

His blood thumped in the sudden silence. He turned at random, blundering through double doors into darkness. He looked up, disoriented, suddenly realizing the single, tarnished silvery light overhead was a poor replica of the moon. And there were stars, though only a scattered few were working. He walked over the uneven imitation of outdoor landscape, feet sinking into the squashy 'earth' and brushing over the plastic grass.

He heard a faint sound across the chamber from him and stopped to listen. 'Stop, wait for me,' he shouted.

Silence again, in the synthetic moonlight casting his faint grey shadow on the ground.

He moved on again, getting nervous, hunting for a way out of the near-darkness. Another sound, to his right; this time he didn't speak, started moving quickly toward it. A shuffling footstep, behind him. He stopped, tense and alert, not knowing which way to go.

Suddenly the double doors crashed open and light flooded in. A click, sharp crack and flash, and he stumbled backwards, at first disbelieving, then running and colliding with the wall simultaneously with a second gunshot. He groped for a door, emergency exit, found the handle, stumbled through into another chamber.

Lights were dim but he could make out a vast total experience auditorium, aisles of seats curving like ploughed furrows across the floor, the stage at one side, white and empty. Nowhere to hide; he ran across the auditorium, glancing behind him, eyes swimming with after images from the flash of the gunshot, ears singing. His footsteps echoed in the wide empty hall.

He stumbled through another door and too late realized that it led into darkness. But he ran on and then screamed in reflex as the floor vanished and he fell dropping terrified through empty darkness for a little eternity until he flopped sickeningly into a deep pile of plastic billowing up like froth and feathers. Typical pleasure palace trick; the foam was ten feet thick, he floundered and sank helplessly at each attempted step.

But then from above, sounds of his pursuers. The door

opened and a light searched around, finally shining down the shaft into which he'd fallen. He glimpsed a shadowy figure above him. But the light had given him a glimpse of the way out and he managed to roll off the foam and on to solid floor. Through another door.

Twenty images of himself ran toward him, saw him, stopped and looked dazedly around. Trapped in a multi-faced prism; the glass surfaces were on each side, above and below; 3D mirror maze. His stupidly bewildered, panicky face was everywhere. He hit a glass screen, side-stepped, fell forward down glass stairs across a depthless crystal mosaic, ran into a mirror, blundered around more panels and down more stairs.

Then from up and behind him, another gunshot, and two more. Glass shattered on all sides and fragments tumbled down through the maze from one level to the next, a shimmering avalanche tinkling as panels caved in and sprinkled debris over the glass floor. Johnson searched around but he could still see only himself. He kicked, kicked harder, and mirrors caved in. Glass splintered and at last he found the exit.

On the Powerpath

Outside. The cold air hit him and he shivered, confused by intersecting ramps and stairways connecting the shopping levels. He ran down a long curving strip of concrete, under tinted plastic roofing, past walls decorated in coloured ceramics, buildings overhead crowding the sky, toweringly claustrophobic.

He reached the front of the pleasure palace and stopped, seeing a face peering round a corner ahead. But then he realized it was Vincent. The loner beckoned and Johnson hurried up; wordlessly, Vincent led him through a side alley, down to understreet service channels and into an underground bay where giant zinc plated refuse disposal bins glinted dully above them in the shadows.

Amanda and Reid were there. Johnson leant weakly against the base of one of the metal bins. He was trembling, near exhaustion, breathing too fast to talk.

'Why the panic?' said Vincent.

'Civics – civics almost got me again.'

'They tried for us as well,' Vincent said. 'Set up a trap, but we knew the pleasure palace better than they did.'

'The way you disappeared, we almost thought you'd set it up for us,' Reid said grimly.

'If you don't believe they were after me, shot at me . . .' Johnson began.

Vincent looked at the civic. He was still breathing hard, clothes askew, glass fragments caught in his thinning hair. He looked confused and scared. The loner smiled faintly. 'I believe you.'

'Can't we get away now?' Amanda said. 'Now. Before they find us again.'

'And leave this bastard behind for them,' said Reid.

'No. He comes with us.'

'They'd leave us alone if they had him to take home with them.'

'We don't know. Civics have never meddled with us before, they've never come into the lone zones. We need to find out why. If Johnson's important to them, he's important to us.' He took hold of the civic's arm. 'We'll try the high-level powerpath. Get as far as possible before sun-set.'

They walked in single file, Vincent leading, Johnson behind him followed by Amanda and Reid. They threaded their way through the alleys and back streets, winding up and round the massive complex of buildings and finally emerging on to an elevated pedestrian way, built to transport several hundred thousand citizens daily in and out of the centremart, on foot at rooftop level.

Except for demonstration tests and adjustments soon after its completion, the powerpath had never been used. Its interleaved steel plates lay gathering grime, patterned with ice reflecting the colours of the sky.

They walked in silence for hours through the afternoon, until the sun began to set ahead of them. High clouds, stretching in ragged parallel streamers spanning the sky, caught the evening sunlight and shone like a broad rainbow, softest blue-violet overhead merging into phosphorescent green and orange and deepest red at the darkening horizon.

The tall apartment blocks, empty and dead but magnificent in their stark, bare symmetry, passed either side in unending regular succession, tinted chrome yellow and ochre where they faced west, but lost in grey shadow where their walls looked away from the sun.

The powerpath terminated in a suburban transfer station and the loners led Johnson across to a nearby monorail track, unused and thick with powdery rust. Three feet wide, the rail paralleled several others leading deeper into the suburban zones.

Walking along it, Johnson was at first unnerved by the forty-foot drop either side. But as the sunlight faded and the shadows deepened in the cold stillness of the evening, the track came to seem alone and unrelated to its surroundings, a snaking red-brown strip floating on volumes of grey-dark space, leading through the city under the black sky.

Fatalists

When it was completely dark and they had walked almost fifteen miles, Vincent led the way off the track down a service ladder to the ground.

'Not our usual area,' he told Johnson. 'Nothing here except apartment blocks. These monorail tracks don't connect with civic centres; they're not through lines, they end in a lone zone residential area. So there's no reason for civics to use them, ever. We should be safe now.'

They found a small food store and Vincent held a flashlight while each person took what he wanted. When

Johnson had gathered his food Vincent went through it weeding out what was likely to be decayed or inedible.

'Eat mainly the irradiated stuff – that'll last for decades yet. Vakpaks, dehydrates, check the plastic seals. If they're broken, it'll poison you.'

'You only live on packaged food? I should have thought that vitamin deficiencies would . . .'

Vincent briefly turned the flashlight on himself. He stood nine inches taller than the stooped civic. He was weather-tanned, clear-eyed, firm-fleshed and casually strong. 'We get all the vitamins, trace minerals and the rest in pills and capsules. We take what we need. Most packaged food was synthesized to contain all the necessary vitamins, in any case. We eat what we need. We live outdoors. We don't let anything worry us. Who's healthier, you or me?'

Johnson felt suddenly inferior, pale-skinned, ageing and weak, though hardly older than the loner. 'Are you going to tell me you have children, as well?' he said.

Vincent shrugged. 'Some do. Most don't, by choice. Probably we're more fertile than the civics; but probably our birth rate's even lower. Having children makes no sense when they'll have nothing to live on. Even irradiated food won't outlast a century. And what would children have to live for? We're a one-generation people, Johnson, and we face it, we learn to live with the city instead of trying to fight circumstances. More than you've done.'

'At least civics hold some hope . . .'

'Not for themselves. For the future. That's too abstract for me.'

Johnson sighed. 'Both there's always some faint chance we could have it both ways – restore the birth rate somehow, without sacrificing civilized life. That's what civics are dedicated to.'

Vincent shrugged. 'Lost cause. You can't reverse history. Man built, the cities; as though sensing the need for an addictive drug never before synthesized. The cities destroyed man; they fed his intellect for a while, but ruined him biologically, psychologically. The most you can do now is delay the end, keep having a few children so each generation struggles on in the ruins, more and more inbred, weaker, unable to think for itself, decaying as the buildings decay. It'll happen. It's happening. It's inevitable. You should face it.'

'Fatalism . . .'

'Realism.'

Suddenly bored with the conversation, Vincent turned to Reid and Amanda, standing waiting in the shadows. 'Let's sleep here,' he said.

'I was going to suggest it,' Reid answered.

'There are empty apartments all round us,' Johnson protested.

'We don't know this area,' said Vincent. 'Sometimes you'll find people who've lived isolated for years, they're insane, they see a stranger and the first thing they do is try to kill him. Safer to stay here, now it's dark.'

They ate their meal of food concentrates and mixes, tasteless and mushy but filling. Afterwards, Amanda asked Johnson if he needed anything done for the wounds from his fall. At first he distrusted her.

'Why are you so suddenly concerned?'

She smiled, her face calm and serene, but puzzled, as if it ought to be obvious to him. 'Why should I withhold help from you? There'll be first aid tins somewhere in the supermart if you need them. Do you?'

He tentatively touched the cuts on his forehead. They were healing. 'It'll be all right,' he said.

She smiled briefly, turned back to where she'd been sitting beside Vincent and put her arm round him, bending to kiss him. But he muttered something to her and gestured, and she went over to Reid, who'd said little and kept to himself all day except for occasional hard, resentful glances at Johnson.

At first Reid shook his head and wouldn't look at Amanda. Johnson watched the two figures in the darkness and heard murmured words; finally she took Reid's hand and he stood up after her, both of them walking further into the supermart; out of sight in the shadows of an aisle half blocked with fallen packets of soap powder.

In the silence of the place Johnson heard the rustle of clothes, more whispered words, and heavier breathing slowly leading up to love making.

He shifted uncomfortably, pulled some cartons down and spread them out on the floor, found a display of bath sponges and made a rough bed and pillow from them. Vincent was still sitting, watching him quietly.

'Are you waiting for something?' Johnson said.

'Just looking at you,' came the slow, easy reply. 'Trying to see how you could ever imagine you'd fit into our kind of life.'

Johnson paused carefully. 'It's too early to tell,' he said. 'I don't altogether understand how you live, yet.'

'You need to understand it? You make it sound a problem, a challenge. It's the easiest way of life there is; why not just accept it? All you have to do is relax and take it easy.'

Johnson shook his head. 'I can't be as casual as that. Neither are you, underneath. Your fatalism, the way you pretend not to worry about anything, it doesn't seem to stop you being aware of life, the social situation. You've thought it out logically, you're not just a tramp, wasting his life away.'

Vincent sighed. 'You miss the point. So I'm educated; self-educated. Why not? I'm intelligent, there are many libraries. I care about some things; the group, our freedom, the city. But just because I care doesn't mean I get hung up on it, like you do. Civics are always dissatisfied, when they care, because they always see it could be better. Nothing's ever perfect.'

'Obviously. How could it be?'

Vincent laughed. 'Life is as it is, perfect or imperfect, and if you'd stop fighting it and accept it as it is, you wouldn't worry any more about making it better. There just isn't any point. We're at the end of the road.'

'That's a hopeless outlook, when one still can change things, alter the environment, work to make it better.'

'Sure, men have never done anything else. And this is how it ended, with the cities, the ultimate environment providing everything one needs except solitude or peace of mind. But we loners have even got that, now. Wouldn't you say that's a fortunate position? In all the history of mankind, we're the first generation to live in harmony with our man-made environment. The last generation, too. We're enjoying it.'

Vincent was smiling. Johnson angrily shook his head. 'This is so decadent . . .'

'Do you want to start on ethics? We have our own ethics.'

'Ethics that encompass fatalism and . . . and polygamy?'

Vincent laughed quietly in the darkness. 'Polyandry, civic, not polygamy. But that's just circumstances; there's a shortage of women so we have to form a three-way relationship. We don't try and fight facts, preserve monogamy like the civics do. We're slummer descendants, remember that; it's in the blood, making do with what we have, accepting what we're given, making it work.'

There was a silence. The moon emerged from behind a cloud and pale light shone in through the deep supermart windows, showing Vincent sitting easily on a section of empty shelving, Johnson huddled in his nest on the floor with sponges and cartons piled up round him.

'You can't tell me you'd be so fatalistic if, say, you were in danger,' the civic said. 'You'd fight it, you'd alter your environment if you could.'

Vincent yawned. 'This is getting trivial. If you jumped me I'd knock you to pieces. If it was an armed party of civics, I'd run. Just because we fit ourselves to situations doesn't mean we don't weigh them up first. And now it's bed-time, civic; think things over. Try it our way. It's easier.' He shot Johnson one last, hard look. 'And don't hold out on me. You're keeping something hidden and I don't like that. Soon you're going to have to tell me what it is.'

Vincent vanished into the darkness. Johnson lay on his

lumpy bed and stared out of the window for a long time at the changing sky, moonlight patterning the clouds. The last sounds he heard before he drifted into sleep were more rustlings of clothes, whispers and sounds of love from the neighbouring aisle. Vaguely he wondered if it were Reid or Vincent with the woman. But did it matter?

The Old Woman

Johnson woke with something smothering him. He struggled, opened his eyes, then saw it was Vincent's hand pressed down over his mouth.

The loner saw Johnson was awake. 'Don't speak,' he whispered quietly, lifting his hand from the civic's face. 'And don't move.'

Johnson felt the floor trembling faintly. He turned his head a little until he could just see out of the supermart front windows. On the monorail, a train was edging past, grinding and rumbling along the rusty track.

It passed out of sight and Vincent stood up. He motioned Johnson to follow him and they went to the back of the store where Reid and Amanda were waiting.

'That track just doesn't lead anywhere. They must be searching for us, still.' He glanced at Johnson. 'They must want you pretty bad, to come so far, following someone who just wrote a letter.'

Their eyes met. Johnson looked back at the loner, saying nothing. Vincent turned away. 'I still don't want a face-to-face with them,' he went on. 'But we ought to have weapons for self-defence if nothing else.'

Reid sighed. 'I don't like running from civics.'

Vincent shrugged. 'I don't like being massacred by civics. We go hunting these ones, there'll be ten times as many coming into the lone zone looking for us.'

'There's a sports shop that stocks guns in the next shopping centre along, isn't there?' said Amanda.

Vincent nodded. 'Probably looted, but we'll try it.'

They left by the back exit, climbing over tumbled heaps of cardboard boxes. Outside, the cold air was sharp and painful, biting into skin, making eyes water. The wind was strengthening, heavy grey-black clouds hanging low over the apartment blocks.

'Snow this afternoon,' Amanda said.

They zig-zagged through back streets away from the monorail line but often unable to avoid the wide, desolate, main boulevards where the wind funnelled down and swept between the parallel faces of the buildings, drawing the last traces of warmth and moisture from Johnson's reddening hands and face. He felt isolated and vulnerable in the wide streets, even when close to the buildings. The blocks were bleak, withdrawn, coldly hostile in the emptiness, offering no comfort or security. To be a moving figure in this giant concrete graveyard was to feel pitifully insignificant, no right to be alive in the midst of such deadness.

Vincent abruptly motioned the rest of them to stop. They stood a moment, silent and waiting. 'What is it?' asked Johnson.

'Life up ahead. Little signs – discarded food pack, clean curtains in the window there.' He pointed to the top floor of the block in front of them.

They followed him as he walked round the side of the building. 'This is all we needed,' Vincent said. He sighed. 'You saw which room,' he said to Reid. 'Take Amanda with you up one set of stairs. I'll go with Johnson up the others. Approach from opposite ends of the top floor corridor, right?'

Reid nodded. They walked into the entrance hall of the block. Vincent pointed to regular tracks of footprints through the dust on the floor. 'Permanent resident,' he said. 'Two of them.'

They split into pairs and started climbing the emergency stairs.

'Why do we have to go through all this?' asked Johnson.

'Remember what I said last night? People in these backwater areas, old men and women who moved in when the lone zone was first built, just before the crisis – they aren't like loners, always moving on. They make a permanent home, they get so's they can't stand the thought of strangers. Friend of mine once got shot in the back for just walking past some old bastard's apartment window. You've got to check. It's the only way.'

'What if whoever-it-is turns out to be friendly?'

'We'll warn them about the civics and move on.'

They reached the top floor. Vincent led the way to the front corridor. There were more tracks in the dust. Amanda and Reid came into view at the other end of the passage, and the four of them met together and paused outside the door of the inhabited apartment.

Vincent thumped on the panels.

They waited, cold and tense in the damp, dim corridor. But there was no sound from inside.

'Loners,' Vincent shouted, 'seeking no violence. Do we find loners?'

It was a ritual phrase, Johnson realized.

There was still no reply. Reid glanced at Vincent. 'I'll do it,' he said, and stepped forward. Vincent, Amanda, and Johnson moved back from the doorway.

Reid reached inside his rough clothing and pulled out a plastic-handled household knife filed and shaped into a throwing dagger. He held it a moment, pausing calmly. Johnson felt his stomach tighten apprehensively, as Reid carefully tried the doorhandle, found it locked, and stepped back.

He kicked out at the door. It splintered, sharp snapping of the panels. He kicked again. The door gave. He barged it and it broke free with a crash and he lunged forward into a room with Vincent and Amanda right after him.

Suddenly a gunshot sharp and deafening and with it a scream quickly falling into agonized groaning. Vincent shouted something. Johnson tumbled into the room, dazed and confused. Reid was sprawled on the floor with arms stretched out in frozen surprise. He was bleeding heavily from his side, moaning, his eyes closed. Amanda bent over him.

Across the room, on an ancient rocking chair filched from God knew where, a yellow-skinned old woman sat slumped back, eyes vacant, blood pulsing from where Reid's knife had lodged deep in her neck. The rifle she'd used to shoot him still lay in her lap and the rocking chair tilted slowly back and forth, back and forth, while her blood flowed down the old varnished wood and dripped into a pool on the polished concrete floor.

Vincent was swearing, hand on forehead, watching Amanda trying to cover Reid's wound.

'Look for bandages, anything,' she said.

Vincent pushed past Johnson, who was standing weakly against the wall. The loner searched fruitlessly in the kitchenette and then turned out the cupboard in the bedroom. They heard him mutter with surprise.

He came back and flung a yellow-white dress down on the floor beside Amanda. It was an ancient, rotting wedding gown, decades old. Amanda started tearing it into strips.

'Crazy old woman,' Vincent said, glancing at the figure slumped in the rocking chair. He stared grimly at her.

Then, stiffly, as if holding himself rigid, he turned away shaking his head slowly from side to side.

Johnson went into the bedroom and came back with a bed sheet. 'Can I cover her up?'

No one bothered to answer. He turned and draped the sheet over the staring, hollow-cheeked face and emaciated old body muffled in tattered clothes.

On the floor, Reid was breathing in agonized, shallow gasps. Blood had already soaked through the improvised bandage. Amanda's face was pale under its tan.

'We'll have to stay with him,' she said. 'No more moving on.'

Vincent nodded. 'Then I'll go and find food, a medikit, guns too, if possible. I'll be back as soon as I can.'

She forced a faint smile at him; he put his hand on her

shoulder and looked down at her a moment before striding out of the apartment.

Silence closed in; the room filled with Reid's painful breathing. Johnson shifted uneasily; the cold, cramped apartment was like a tomb. He glanced out of the tiny window.

'It's snowing,' he said irrelevantly.

Amanda didn't answer. She stayed crouched over Reid on the floor, staring blankly down at him, watching the blood welling up and flowing easily through each new dressing as she applied it.

Civic Attack

They waited for fifteen long, silent minutes while outside the snow fell more and more heavily, a drifting white slow-motion waterfall colouring everything misty monochrome grey under the heavy sky of black clouds.

Johnson, slumped down on the floor with his back against the cold white wall, found his thoughts sluggish and unformed, incapable of assimilating or reacting to the meaning of the situation. There was a limit, he realized to the amount of change one could respond to; beyond a certain point the mind acted impartially like a computer, taking in and storing information, with no emotional accompaniment. Only days later would he be able to realize the full sensory impact of the events which had taken place around him. For the time being he would have to exist on reflexes alone.

He looked up as Amanda shifted her position for the first time, standing up and wiping her hair out of her face.

'He's going to die,' she said quietly, not looking at him. The words came out flat and resigned and they said all there was to be said. She sat on one of the plastic dining chairs and stared blankly at the opposite wall. 'There's nothing more I can do.'

Johnson licked his hard frost-cracked lips with his dry tongue. Numbing coldness from the concrete floor was gradually creeping up his legs. 'You – you sound as if it's hopeless, as if you don't care any more.'

Her eyes moved to rest steadily, sadly on him. Slowly, she shook her head. 'If he's going to die, I can't stop that.'

'You can fight it.'

'Only so far. Beyond that, fate – God – destiny – whatever you call it – takes over.'

Her eyes were deep with sadness, defeat. Johnson looked away, down at the dust on the floor. Under the old woman's rocking chair, the pool of blood had darkened and congealed.

The silence broke then, with a sharp echoing crack from down in the street outside. Then a volley, gunfire resounding between the buildings.

Johnson scrambled up and hurried to the window, but the snow was falling so thickly he couldn't see the street at all.

Amanda sat motionless, closing her eyes. 'Not him as well,' she murmured.

Silence closed in again.

'I could go down to the entrance hall,' Johnson said.

'Stay here.'

They waited.

At last, distant footsteps sounded, running nearer. Amanda got up and pulled the sheet back, picking the old woman's rifle off her lap, loading it from ammunition still clutched in the dead figure's hand.

Amanda turned to face the doorway with the gun, as the running footsteps sounded in the corridor. But it was Vincent who appeared in the doorway, half falling into the room, snow in his hair and on his clothes, a .22 rifle under one arm, medical supplies under the other.

Amanda dropped her gun and ran to him.

'Civic bastards out there must have followed us all the way,' Vincent gasped. 'Tried to pick me off but the snow makes it hard to see. I think I hit one of them but couldn't tell. We must get out fast, there are scores of them. We'd never hold out, trapped in here. Get this on Reid, and hurry.'

Amanda pulled back the blood-saturated bandages and sprayed quick-drying antiseptic sealant over the wound with swift, urgent strokes. He moaned and tried to turn over, then slumped back.

'I don't think it's any use,' she said.

'Certain?'

'He's lost so much blood. He's hurt so badly, he can't travel . . .'

Vincent groaned and held his forehead; it was too much to bear. 'We – we'll have to leave him,' he said.

Johnson stood up. 'But you *can't* . . .'

Vincent looked at him angrily, tanned face a confusion of rage and helpless despair. 'Be lucky if *any* of us get away, civic. Can't let a dead man hold us back.'

'He's not dead!'

'He will be if he's moved. All right, do what you want, civic. No time. Each for himself now.'

Amanda stood up, glanced one last time at Reid, then hurried after Vincent out into the corridor. Johnson hesitated, then bent down and laboriously hoisted unconscious Reid across his shoulder. He straightened up, staggering with the weight, then stumbled out along the corridor following the loners.

Vincent had stopped at the end. He glanced at Johnson and waved him back.

'Too late. Civics in the building.' Footsteps were pounding up the emergency stairs. 'It'll have to be the roof.'

They turned back, hurried to a short flight of steps leading up to a red door. Vincent pushed it open and they followed him up and out.

The snow hit them, swirling white and wet and icy cold. Johnson gasped and almost dropped Reid. Vincent pushed him aside, took out a knife and cut two wedges from the wooden stock of his rifle. He used the butt to bang the wedges in at the top and bottom of the roof access door.

'This is crazy,' Johnson said. 'We're trapped here, can't get across to another building, those wedges won't hold anyone back for long . . .'

'Take off your clothes,' Vincent snapped, already unzipping his own. 'Knot them together, into a rope.'

'We're fifteen storeys up!'

'Do it!'

Johnson laid Reid down in the snow on the roof and started following Vincent's command. He glanced around at the heavy white snow, curtaining off visibility. The square platform of the flat roof was totally isolated in grey space.

Naked to the waist, with white flakes melting and running over his pale shivering body, Johnson handed his clothes to Vincent, who was already knotting Amanda's together. He finally looped the knotted garments around the parapet rail and slung them down over the side.

There were sounds of footsteps on the stairs up to the emergency door. Someone tried it. Shouts. More running feet.

Vincent swung over the parapet and shinned down out of sight. He balanced outside the window of an apartment on the floor below, smashed it with his fist, groped inside and opened the catch, and swung into the room.

'Amanda,' he called up to her. 'Quickly!'

She didn't hesitate, climbed on the parapet, disappeared out of sight.

The thumps on the emergency door were getting louder and more purposeful.

Johnson dragged Reid to the edge, picked him up and lowered him down. Blood droplets from the wound fell with the white snowflakes, disappearing out of sight to the street fifteen floors below.

'Take him from me, for God's sake,' Johnson called. 'It's the least you can do.'

From the window below, Vincent grudgingly reached out and hauled in the unconscious figure.

Then Johnson, trembling with cold, climbed over and down the rough rope, fingers numb and unfeeling, naked in the snowstorm, hanging over the sickening drop to the street.

His feet touched the window sill, slipped, touched again, his hands lost their grip and he cried out falling into the room and cutting himself on broken glass from the window. They'd abandoned Reid on the floor. Johnson couldn't tell if he was dead or alive but he picked him up anyway and staggered gasping after Vincent and Amanda, now hurrying along the corridor, while overhead the civic police were pouring out on to the roof.

'Have to risk the elevator,' Vincent said, holding the doors back. Johnson staggered in. 'If that corpse overloads us, I'll kill you,' Vincent said, thumbing the button.

Rusty machinery ground protestingly, the doors edged half shut, Vincent kicked them and they slid into place. The elevator shuddered, trembled, then sank squealing and rumbling down its shaft to the bottom.

They got the doors open and hurried out across the hallway. Vincent stopped when he saw a figure waiting outside the entrance.

He gestured them back and then crept up on the man, a civic left to guard the block. Vincent sprang on him from behind, felling him, clubbing him with his rifle. He hesitated, then hoisted the unconscious civic on to his back and beckoned Amanda after him.

Why the guard, why not Reid? Johnson wondered, staggering under his own burden of the wounded loner. But there was no time to consider it. They ran out through the snow, slipping and stumbling, dodging into the blizzard. Shouts from behind, muffled by the curtain of white flakes; then gunshots. Terrified, Johnson struggled to keep up. Bullets knocked holes in the surrounding buildings. Johnson saw the unconscious guard across Vincent's shoulders get hit; the man's body twitched and blood spread out from the wound.

Then they turned a corner and ran at random through back streets and alleys while the voices of the pursuers rose and fell behind them. They stopped in the middle of the road, buildings tall sinister grey masses rising up out of sight each side, and Vincent bent down, tugging at something under the snow.

'No hope of losing them when they can follow our footprints,' he said. 'Sewer's the only escape route.'

He pulled up the cover and Amanda climbed quickly down a ladder inside. Vincent passed the civic guard down to her. Johnson came last of all, lowering Reid and then pulling the manhole cover shut above him.

Faintly they heard civics shouting and running nearer, then passing, fading into the distance.

Sewer Interrogation

Vincent had emptied his pockets before taking his clothes off on the roof. So he still had his flashlight. The moist walls of the sewer glittered in a shifting halo as the loner hurried along, turning from one branch of the eight-foot concrete pipe to the next, the others splashing after him.

They rested, finally, when they'd run for about half a mile.

'Civics can't follow us this far,' Vincent said. 'We've taken so many turnings, it'd take hours to track us.'

The dank smell of the pipe was making them all cough, and the noise rang echoing along the walls with the rasping sighing of heavy breathing. Muddy waters flowed slowly along the pipe bottom, chilling their feet. The darkness and the smallness of Vincent's light accentuated the oppressive sensation of weight piled above their heads, great buildings, concrete, and soil pressing down.

Johnson had laid Reid down against the sewer wall. Vincent bent to examine him.

'How is he?' asked Amanda, without any expectancy in her voice.

'Dead,' Vincent replied, equally flatly. 'Impossible for him to live through that.'

'I had to *try* to save him,' Johnson said.

'Thanks,' Vincent said dourly. 'You helped. To reduce

our chances.' He turned to the other wounded man, the civic guard, lying bleeding from where he'd been shot in the back.

'Let's see if this bastard can still talk,' Vincent murmured. 'It's the only reason I brought him with us.' He shone his light in the man's face; the civic's eyes were open, showing pain and fear.

'Hurt bad?' asked Vincent. The man nodded weakly. 'You're friends got you.'

The civic grunted. 'Only because of you. All right, what do you want with me?'

Vincent smiled faintly. 'We'll make a bargain. We can get you drugs. We can save you, understand? We know our way through the sewers. But if you don't tell me what I want to know, we'll leave you here. Maybe you could crawl around for a while, looking for a way out, but you wouldn't find it. You'd just make dying more painful.'

The civic groaned with pain. 'I don't have a choice. And you know it. So quickly, say what you want.'

'Good.' Vincent turned and swung his light on Johnson. 'Do you recognize him?'

The civic guard half sat up, expression turning from pain to disgust. He glared at Johnson, tried to speak, but slumped back. 'I – I know him.' He coughed. 'He was part of our team, till he – he deserted. Ran off to – to turn loner. With you scum.'

'Johnson was with *you* originally? Civic police exploring our zone?'

'Right.'

'He told us a different story – said you'd been following him since he ran from some civic centre. That you were trying to get him for some offence.'

The guard grimaced, shook his head.

Vincent paused a moment. In the silence they could hear water dripping, trickling underfoot. A cold draught moved continually through the sewer in the darkness.

'Then what are the civics in the lone zone for?' asked Vincent.

'Johnson didn't tell you? Trying to play it both ways, I

guess . . . We were briefed, capture some loners, make 'em tell us where their stronghold was. But it took three days even to spot your group. And Johnson had deserted by then. He could have told you what we wanted, so we had to get you dead or alive, stop you telling all your loner friends what we were after.'

'What *were* you after? Why'd you want to find the loner stronghold?'

The man coughed up some blood. His face was contorted, thrown into deep shadows by the flashlight beam. 'Get me something, got to stop pain . . .'

'Tell me, first.'

'People . . . in civic centres, no women left, more and more boy babies. Had to have women. Keep things going. Only way was to get loners, loner women. Capture your headquarters, your centre, work out from there . . .'

Vincent turned on Johnson. 'You held out on us, civic. I knew there was something you were keeping back. You knew all of this, you were part of it, before you deserted.'

Johnson stuttered nervously. 'I c-couldn't complicate my story, when we first met up. You wouldn't have trusted me at all, if I'd told you everything. I had to say I was some kind of criminal. I just wanted to get along, I'd have left you in peace after a while.'

'You decided not to tell us about the rotten civic scheme you'd been mixed up in.'

'Don't get me wrong,' Johnson protested nervously, 'I wouldn't go along with the plan, that's why I deserted. Crazy, barbaric, end supposed to justify the means – I couldn't support it. But if I'd told you I'd been mixed up in it, you'd never have trusted me. I did what anyone would have done, under the circumstances.'

'I've heard enough,' Vincent cut in.'Stop babbling.' Wearily, then, he turned to Amanda. 'You're all right? You can make it down the river?' The hardness had gone from his voice.

'If we run to keep warm,' Amanda said. 'It's not as cold down here as it was in the snow, but I'm still numb all over.'

'Right. Then let's go.'

'Wait!' the wounded civic shouted. 'You can't leave me, you said . . .'

Vincent turned on him. 'You think you deserve any help from me?'

'We made a deal . . .'

'No deal. You're dying and there's nothing I could do even if I wanted to. Do you think I'd go back up there into the snow, half naked with civics waiting to shoot me down?' He laughed bitterly. 'I never even considered it.'

The two loners turned and started splashing away down the sewer, the light going with them. Johnson got up hurriedly.

'You can help me,' the wounded man shouted. 'Just carry me, to safety, somewhere where they'll find me. Hell, it's not much to ask, you and me were in the same unit together.'

'I can't . . .' Johnson began, eyes on the retreating circle of light.

'Bastard!' the civic guard shouted. 'Worse than loner scum. Leave a man to die when you could save him.'

Johnson stood up, numb and shivering, aching cold. Slowly at first, then running, slipping and stumbling in the slimy-bottomed pipe, he started after the loners, the sparkling circle of light at the focus of his awareness.

The Ruined Café

After he'd caught up with Vincent and Amanda it took an hour of stumbling, naked running to reach the end of the sewer. At first eight feet wide, it broadened to ten, finally fifteen feet as more and more tributary pipes joined it and the sludge-choked bottom became deeper and deeper in water. They swam the last length, carried by the current, no longer caring for their frozen flesh and cramped, coughing lungs.

Finally, miraculously, they emerged into the light of

late afternoon, on the bank of a wide, shallow river choked with weeds and vegetation weighed down with chunky, uneven white snow drifts.

Vincent led the way up the slippery bank; he helped Amanda over a concrete parapet and then went up and over himself, glancing back briefly at Johnson but leaving the civic to scramble up on his own.

They found themselves on a wide, snow-covered riverside road, six miles further south in the lone zone. Tall, close-spaced, expensive residential blocks faced the road, separated from it by a narrow line of unkempt trees. The snowfall, now over, had left the city softer, gently rounded, drifts curving up to the buildings and outlining the smallest flat surface. The clouds were clearing, and intermittent sunlight brought the scene to life, the starkness of the buildings accentuated still more by the outlines of shining, sparkling white.

Johnson followed the loners along the road. They were too tired and too beaten to pay him any attention; he walked with them in silence. They stopped at a clothing shop and pulled off the last of their waterlogged clothes, drying themselves and taking garments from the window display to muffle themselves against the cold.

'We must stop soon,' said Amanda. 'I'm exhausted.'

'Just a little further,' said Vincent. 'A square of parkland, remember it? Café in the centre. Plastic red tables. We can make a fire, sleep there. Right.'

She nodded weakly. 'I don't want to risk another apartment.'

Trekking through the snow-carpeted streets was tiring, but warming, now that they had clothes. They stopped once more, this time to pick up food, and then reached the small park, a block given over to flat grassland.

By the entrance was a children's playground, angular shapes of the slides and swings draped in snow that clung like flesh on the awkward bones of metal skeletons. The snow hid everything, but Johnson knew that, underneath it, the playground was as virgin and unused as the rest of the city. He looked away from it as they passed.

The café was a tangled mess of self-service aisles, tables crowded together under a faceted clear-plastic roof that had fallen in, in the centre.

While Vincent broke up furniture to use for a fire, Amanda huddled down on a chair in the corner, saying nothing, avoiding Johnson's eyes.

Vincent tore some labels off cans and used a pocket burning glass to focus the dim sunlight outside and ignite the bright-coloured paper. With it he lit plastic, then the wooden legs from the broken chairs, and soon the garish café walls were flickering and moving to the light from an open fire, crackling and spitting, the smoke rising and puthering under the ceiling before wafting through the broken roof.

This was the end point, Johnson realized. This was how it would be, when the power failed in all the lone zones, when the water became too dissipated with leaks and pipe bursts ever to reach the proper outlets, when leaking gas mains had exhausted the vast natural reservoirs, and when the last of the food finally decayed. Then, there would be nothing to do but burn wood for warmth and light, and kill the animals that had already started invading the cities from surrounding green spaces. Guns would kill them first, then knives, stones, spears . . . But would anyone still be alive, that far ahead?

There had to be a way out; he couldn't face such a decline with the loners' uncaring fatalism. But neither could he be a civic, rigidly bound to preserve a static system organized with the sole aim of reconstructing city life as it had once been.

Vincent had finished building the fire. He sat down beside Amanda, staring dully into the patterns of the flames.

Vincent sighed. He glanced at Johnson. 'Reid was right. I was wrong. We should have left you where we found you.'

'You can't hold me responsible for everything that . . .'

'What's happened, had to happen', Amanda said dully.

'It would probably have turned out this way, whether we'd left Johnson or not.'

'Maybe,' Vincent said. 'I thought we could even gain something from you, civic. Broaden our outlook. But you told us nothing and knifed us in the back.'

'I didn't . . .'

'You shortened our chances all the way along.'

'You're no one to talk of chances, when there was a chance to save Reid.'

There was an abrupt, uneasy silence. Vincent stared back hard at the civic. 'Reid couldn't have been saved,' he said carefully, holding himself under control.

'There *was* a chance, to save a life, when there are so few left to save.'

'He's dead now.'

'What's that got to do with . . .'

'It's a fact, damn it, not a possibility. Can't you tell the difference? Can't you ever face facts? You act like an idiot and expect us to thank you for it.'

'I don't expect . . .'

'Don't you see it's pointless to talk?' Amanda cut in. 'You aren't even using the same language. We deal in realities; you keep coming back to what's right or wrong, what should be, not what is. Your way of thinking makes people keep trying to fight depopulation when there's no hope of changing it. You fight lost causes, you try to save dead men. And you use any means to achieve what you deem worthwhile.'

'Like capturing loner girls and abducting them to the city,' Vincent said. 'It still sounds hardly possible.'

'I find it as unthinkable as you do,' said Johnson. 'But I understand the outlook. To civics, loners are betraying humanity, by living off the past and not caring about the future. Loners are seen as little more than vermin. This plan was a way of forcing them to help preserve the human race.'

'You should never have deserted,' Vincent said. 'You may not be quite as bad as most civics. But you're still one of them. Never one of us.'

Johnson subsided into silence, sitting on his own, the other side of the fire from the loners.

Vincent, his tanned flesh coloured deeper brown by the orange flames, turned and picked a vakpak from his pile of food, slit it with his teeth and handed it to Amanda. He took another for himself, silently and grimly. Johnson just sat and watched. There was nothing to be said.

The Frozen City

The next day, the sky was clear, deep blue and the sun shone down clean and bright through the café's transparent roof.

Achingly stiff, Johnson turned painfully, waking up where he'd spent the night on the bare café floor. He winced as chilblains and sores on his body rubbed against the tough, fibrous clothes in which he'd muffled himself. He had slept eleven hours but felt groggy rather than refreshed.

'We've been waiting, civic,' Vincent's voice said from behind him.

Johnson looked round. The loner was standing in the café doorway, bronze skin gleaming in the bright sun. He stood tall and healthy, clear-eyed, face composed with no trace of the bitterness and depression he had shown the previous night. Johnson, white-skinned like an awkward slug trapped in his thick clothing, squirmed round and struggled upright, stooped, aching and sore, his mouth tasting filthy.

'I wanted to leave you here asleep,' Vincent said. 'But Amanda said we should wait for you to wake up, then take you to the nearest civic centre route. You can get home by yourself.'

'I can't return to a centre.'

'Then wander round on your own. We're through with you.'

He followed Vincent to the door, still half asleep, tripping over the confusion of chairs and tables. Amanda was waiting outside.

The park was a wilderness of sparkling snow, gasping white, glaring blinding bright in the morning-fresh sun. Johnson blinked, dazzled, his eyes watering. He followed the loners across the thick snow, retracing their tracks of the previous afternoon.

Vincent kicked at the snow, sending it flying and drifting like translucent white dust, shimmering as it dispersed on the wind. 'Absurd that no one ever built over this space,' he said quietly.

'People thought that small grassed parks would make city life more bearable,' said Johnson.

Vincent grimaced. 'That's like admitting men were meant for green space, but building cities for them just the same. Putting little parks in was just a token gesture, to save the planners' consciences.'

'For children, it made a difference, grass is nicer . . .'

'Crap. Open your eyes, civic.' The loner gestured at the pattern of concrete buildings surrounding the park. The square structures were laced with snow-festooned, delicate curving ramps and walkways, sun-glittering, ice-bright, splitting the spectrum into twinkling reds, oranges, and mauves that shifted and flashed as they walked past. Deep abysses of shadow, intersected soaring mosaics of pure white shining sterile snow-etched concrete, dwarfing the dark, drab figures of the men walking beneath.

'Did you ever see open countryside as beautiful as this?' Vincent said, openly and naturally, striding easily past the giant structures standing frozen and timeless like sharp-edged rocks naked in the sun.

Ahead, Johnson saw monorail tracks bridging the street.

'We'll leave you soon,' said Amanda.

He said nothing as they started walking up concrete steps transformed into gentle ripples in the covering of smooth drifted snow, like a frozen waterfall. At the top of the steps they paused where a walkway led between the buildings. Johnson walked to the guard rail and looked down to where the monorail tracks ran ten feet below, parallel to the walkway, elevated above the ground lying still farther below in complete shadow. The tracks caught the sunlight, sparkling strips of white twisting between the buildings, suspended over blackness.

'I'm sorry it didn't work out,' Johnson said, not looking round.

'It couldn't.'

'I guess I'll try to live on my own.' He sighed, turning round, moving to his right. He hadn't realized that Vincent had come up beside him. Clumsily, he bumped into the loner, and fell off-balance on to one foot, clutching Vincent's sleeve for support.

His foot slipped on the snow and he lurched over hitting the ground hard, feeling stupid and awkward and angry with himself, then realizing that Vincent was falling too, pushing Johnson further down. And then the civic's awkwardness turned to surprised fear as he fell against the rusted iron guard rail and the old metal buckled and broke in a shower of powdery snow.

For one second Johnson teetered on the edge, staring down helplessly at the monorail tracks in the chasm below him. Then, crying out, his arms waving futilely to keep his lost balance, he toppled forward, tumbling out of control, biting into his lower lip, seeing the tracks suddenly rush up to him.

The jolt as he hit the three-feet-wide metal rail jarred his teeth into his tongue and smacked his legs into a mass of pain. He gasped and croaked, for a moment paralysed, his diaphragm numb. Eyes watering, he clutched the monorail with both arms and looked back up to where Vincent and Amanda were still standing by the broken railings.

'You – You pushed me!' he shouted. 'You did it on purpose!'

Vincent laughed. 'You fell, and you know it.' He paused. 'What are you going to do now – wait for a train?'

Johnson looked down and suddenly saw what was behind Vincent's comment. The monorail he'd landed on was the only one not covered by snow. The steel shone bright and clear, rust free, in regular daily use.

And then, as if to confirm what he'd already realized, he felt the rail beginning to vibrate under him. It was the morning train coming, on its way from southern civic centre through the lone zone to the centre further north.

'Quick, he called. 'There's a train coming now. Reach down to me, and I can get up off the rail.'

Vincent stared down thoughtfully. For a long moment he did nothing. Then, slowly and deliberately, he put his hands in his pockets.

Johnson glanced quickly around. The concrete wall up to the walkway ten feet above, from where he'd fallen, was smooth and unscalable – unless the loners reached down to pull him up. To the other side of Johnson, the next monorail track would offer a refuge. But it was three yards away, separated unreachably over the ground lost in shadow far below. He could never jump the gap.

'I – I tried to help you,' Johnson shouted. 'Please, the least you can do . . .'

'We owe you nothing,' said Vincent.

The rail was vibrating harder under him. The train couldn't be far off.

'Amanda,' he shouted. 'You can help me. It won't cost you anything, I won't bother you any more after this. All you have to do is reach down and give me your hand.'

'You fell,' she said. 'By chance, chance alone. It's not for me to interfere.'

He looked round desperately. The nearest service ladder to the ground was two pylons distant; he might not make it before the train came. He didn't even know which way the train was coming; either side of him, the monorail curved round buildings, out of sight.

'Look, I'll help you,' he said quickly. 'I'll go back to the nearest centre, tell them I deserted so I could spy on you, tell them I know where your stronghold is. That's all they're interested in. They'll send out a party and I'll warn you of their route, you can pick them all off . . .'

Vincent's laughter rang off the buildings. 'You'd betray anyone, play it any way, to save yourself. Forget it, Johnson. There *is* no stronghold, no centre of any kind. That's a civic concept we have no need of. We're loners – our independence is our strength.'

'Please! Look, I'm begging you, for God's sake help me, don't you understand, I'll be killed! Please, please help me, you can, you've got to!'

But they just stood relaxed and unmoving, impassively watching him. And for the first time he realized the extent of their indifference. It would barely interest them, let alone distress them, to see him die.

The rail was rumbling under him. If he'd run for the access ladder to start with, he'd have made it. But he'd wasted too much time. He looked up and saw the train rounding the curve fifty yards away. There were mere seconds left.

Desperately he started running along the track, hearing the train braking behind him, but too late, it could never stop in time, he could never reach the ladder down to the ground.

He made a desperate leap for the neighbouring rail, when the train was almost upon him, but it was far out of his reach and he fell free, twisting as he fell, the wind tangling his clothes, the air pressing past his face.

'I tried,' he told himself. 'I wanted to live like them.'

He fell from sun into shadow, grey pillars patterning round him and ground suddenly too close, too close – and then he hit the concrete.

Above him, the train accelerated again, wary of a possible trap set by loners. Vincent and Amanda stood quietly watching the steel cars receding out of sight round the next curve in the track.

Then, their faces composed as if they had already lost all memory of Johnson, they walked away along the glittering, ice-covered powerpath into the glare of the morning sun, past frost-laced walls, over iced puddles reflecting the snow-capped buildings shimmering in the vibrant air, across snow-encrusted bridges and ramps, gleaming and perfect, and along white-carpeted boulevards where the magnificent apartment blocks rose like remote islands lapped at their bases by the undulating snow, lying like a white, wind-caressed sea of frozen time . . .

The loners walked back into their crystallized city, and the world died with them.

PART FOUR

The Last Stages

Years passed in deserted cities across the land, and the broad faces of the tall buildings, once so clean and new, aged and decayed a little more with the passing of each season. In lone zone and civic centre alike, the concrete cracked in winter frost and crumbled in summer sun; brickwork and masonry split and fell into the streets below. Rain and snow dulled the tinted, plastic-panelled façades with streaks of grime, and filmed the wide windows with grey dirt. The massive supermarts, office blocks, and apartment buildings in the uninhabited linear cities settled further on their foundations each year, as did the longer-standing structures in zones where the last of humanity still maintained a pretence of civilization.

All the buildings were crumbling, subsiding, timeworn, and dying. The streets became clogged with fallen rubble, concrete and broken glass, steel sections and plastic sheeting. Rainwater collected in dirty pools where the road asphalt had slowly sunk into deepening hollows.

In all its various forms, the city was worn and crumbling, and had entered the last stage of its own death.

The Bronze Statue

It has been a long, cold night; heavy storm clouds have covered the moon, releasing intermittent showers of fine rain swept on great gusts of wind through the empty streets.

Manning walks quietly along the rust-roughened steel monorail line leading between the tall buildings to what was once a civic centre, fifty years ago. The distinction between civic centre and lone zone is blurred now; as the buildings decay, so they come to look alike. The people, too, cannot be divided into separate groups with separate philosophies. Philosophy has died with the interest in the future; men live only from day to day, in small communities from which they seldom stray.

Manning has been up all night, wandering through the city, but he still feels restless and untouched by sleep. He follows the elevated rail in under the broken roof of the terminus and leaps across to the platform; skirting piles of rubble, he gropes his way to the broken automatic gates, vaults them and walks down the littered treads of an escalator.

Out in the street, he moves slowly and warily, often pausing, scanning the patterns of moonlight and shadow. The long streets are deep, dark canyons; the soot-black buildings tower either side.

A few blocks away, the cars have already assembled in the town square. The roar of their engines echoes through the deserted streets, rising and falling on the wind. Manning walks into an alley choked with mounds of empty cans and food wrappers salvaged from an adjoining supermart warehouse. He scrambles up the refuse heap, reaches the bottom of a fire-escape ladder and pulls himself clear.

Up on the roof, four storeys above, he moves through a jungle of chimney stacks, inspection ladders and rusty catwalks, over a giant ventilation duct and to the front of the building, where he settles himself behind a parapet overlooking the town square.

Six main roads lead into the square. The cars are roaring from one inter-section to the next, veering and turning at random, skidding in tyre-rending powerslides. Exhaust fumes rise and drift in clouds, headlamp beams swing like searchlights over the faces of the aged buildings lining the square.

The cars are stripped of all bodywork, down to the bare skeletal frames. Electric power units have been ripped out and supplanted with high-powered, furious petrol-burning V8 engines gathered from refuse dumps and long-forgotten spare part stores.

The drivers are hunched forward, shouting to each other over the bellowing exhaust noise and the wailing car horns.

Opposite Manning, across the square, the old town hall stands in shadow, its deep windows and tall columns coated with grime. A bronze statue mounted on a massive granite pillar, chipped and age-worn, marks the centre of a road junction in front of the building; the cars race wildly round the column, make high speed U-turns and move off again like a shifting swarm of black insects, without pattern or direction.

Footsteps behind Manning suddenly distract him from the scene below. He turns warily, tense and alert, but it is only Wickens out on one of his night walks. The old man, bearded face lit obliquely by the intermittent headlamp glare, sits down in front of the parapet beside Manning and watches the scene silently.

Finally Wickens sighs.

'Just the same as last month. Just the same.'

Manning looks up in vague interest. 'A month?' He fumbles under his ragged raincoat, dragging out an old notebook. 'I suppose so. Maybe less than a month.'

He flicks through the tattered pages as if able to read them in the dark. Then he absent-mindedly turns back to look at the street below, stuffing his book back in his pocket. 'It may be three weeks, Wickens, I don't know.'

'But it's the same, isn't it. Isn't it?'

Manning says nothing.

'Damn you, Manning, *isn't* it the same?'

He looks up, suddenly realizing Wickens wants an answer. 'Why yes. Of course it's the same.'

'Where you been, Manning? Haven't seen you around for a couple of months.'

Manning sighs, forced into conversation. 'I've been with them, sometimes.' He gestures at the people in the cars.

Wickens scowls, 'Wasting your time. It'll happen again the same as before, and you can't stop it, Manning. Restlessness, sleeplessness, then riot night, next week, maybe even sooner, just like before.'

Manning frowns, automatically looking back at the cars. The driving is wilder now. The cars, black silhouettes against white headlamp glare, weave and flash across road junctions, racing one another, paths intersecting at random. Several head simultaneously for the bronze statue from different directions; the first three turn and career off on new paths but the last pair mis-time it. They brake too late, wheels locked and screaming, tyres smoking, skidding broadside.

They impact together at the base of the statue. Metal frames buckle up effortlessly against the granite pillar. Figures pinwheel free, arms outstretched and their screaming mingles with the rending of steel. The two cars crash back down on to the road, headlamps tilted up at the black sky. An engine howls at full throttle before exploding into silence. Flames flower and hiss across petrol leaking over the road.

Other cars converge slowly, circling like inquisitive dirty black flies. One by one they stop; drivers switch off engines, get out and crowd round, their giant shifting shadows projected by car headlamps on to the backdrop of buildings.

A crash victim is still shouting and moaning. Otherwise, it is all suddenly quiet. Manning stands up, limbs cold and numb.

Wickens grunts. 'Time someone put a stop to all this. We've been here for too long. Civics tried to keep it static, preserve the old ways but that can't work, not in the long run. Not now that we've got only a few hundred of us left living here.'

'Yes.'

The old man chews his beard, staring at Manning. 'What d'you mean, "yes"?

Manning sighs. 'Yes, I mean yes, of course, you're right, Wickens, you were right the last time you said all this, and the time before that. But you just go on watching it all run down, complaining, doing nothing. You haven't seen me because I've been with *them*, lately, some older ones as well, people you never meet because they're dull, ordinary, rooted in their homes, stagnating like everyone else. They're going to pieces like the buildings are going to pieces.'

Manning looks away, embarrassed at making so long a speech. But Wickens angrily clutches the younger man's arm, turning him round. 'All right, so what're you doing, Manning, to sort it all out?'

'There may be nothing I can do. But at least I try to understand.'

Wickens sighs in exasperation, starts to speak, but decides it isn't worth it. Without warning he jumps up and slams Manning back against the ventilation duct, seizing his throat with gnarled, wiry fingers and shaking him angrily.

'You never listen. Never! Times I've said, ain't no *use*, trying to understand them. But you, you wander around, talking to them, trying to get something out of people who aren't hardly people no more, you call that . . .'

Manning stands limply letting Wickens shake him to and fro, like an independent witness to his own strangulation. Wickens finally grunts and turns away, wrinkled hands trembling. 'Face it, Manning. It's too late for talking. Everyone's rooted here. Only way to break the pattern is *force* 'em out.'

'What do you mean?'

The old man paused thoughtfully, carefully, as if trying not to say too much. He rattles his archaic false teeth, spits on the roof.

'We both know things'll go on getting worse. Unless we get people out. I seen it happen, men losing all interest in living till they can't see no further than the walls of their houses. A purge, Manning, is what we need.'

'Is that all you're going to say?'

The old man chuckled, chin on chest, involved in some private joke. 'Come round my place sometime. Maybe you'll hear more.' He scratches under his shaggy hair, coughs and turns slowly, sitting down on the parapet again.

Manning nods thoughtfully. He gathers his overcoat more tightly around himself and walks back over the roof, through the shadows.

In the square, the flames are burning lower at the foot of the statue, dimly lighting the bronze figures above. They stand in a stylized family group: two stern-faced parents and their young children, a boy and a girl, innocent-faced, hand in hand.

A century ago, the civics erected the statue to symbolize the formal society they hoped to foster and perpetuate. But now, the blank eyes of the bronze figures stare into twilight over the heads of youths still assembled silently, like some religious congregation, around the pair of wrecked, flaming cars.

The Iron Bridge

Manning has walked away from the square, slowly and wearily through the deserted streets, toward the old library, where he sleeps in a bed made like a rat's nest from pages torn out of an encyclopaedia. The library is his refuge; he sometimes retreats there for days, pacing the shadowy aisles between the tall blocks of bookshelves, playing tapes, reading microfilm.

He seeks solitude instinctively. Born outside this city zone, he has never felt kinship with the people in it. Dressed in ragged trousers and heavy grey sweater under his old raincoat, he is as inconspicuously drab as the weathered buildings; his shoulder-length hair is matted with dirt, and four days' beard roughens his face. He moves slowly and says little, and the youths in their cars accept him as grudgingly as the older people huddled in their subsiding apartment blocks.

Ahead of him, swift-moving clouds are laced with shifting dawn sunlight. He shivers, hungry, cold, achingly tired, yet knowing he cannot sleep. He is still restless, after being awake all night.

He hears a car engine from behind and stops and turns. The stripped-down vehicle is approaching him along the street, weaving between heaps of rubble. Like the others in the square, the car's bodywork is gone; there is only the black, oily chassis. It skids to a stop beside Manning; in it he recognizes Sheldon driving, dressed in red, and Neal beside him, wearing old mechanic's overalls. Neal is Wickens's grandson.

'Manning,' Sheldon shouts, revving the car's unsilenced engine. 'Heading cross river. Come?'

Manning pauses, then shrugs and clambers on the dirty frame, crouching where the back seat has been ripped off. The car accelerates, chassis trembling with power, oil spraying from the transmission, fumes gushing from sawn-off exhaust. At a steady sixty, dodging pot holes and debris, they roar back toward the town square and pass the two wrecked cars still smouldering at the base of the statue.

Sheldon circles round them, tyres screaming. He yells wordlessly.

'Great, last night,' he shouts over his shoulder. 'See all the blood?'

'Exactly how'd it happen?' asks Manning.

'Fire and blood!' Sheldon shouts.

He bangs his hand on the horn and the long, blaring note echoes behind them around the square as they take off down toward the river.

Manning clutches the car frame with numbed fingers as it sways under him. The cold wind bites into his skin, turns hands and face raw red, ripping at his clothes, whipping his hair into his watering eyes. They drive through a sudden rain shower and the wheels throw fountains of spray into the icy air. Manning clenches his teeth and the youths crouch low as the river comes into sight, spanned by an ancient iron bridge hanging over the grey water like a rusty cobweb stretched from bank to bank. The car accelerates, buffeted by sudden gusts, jumping over the uneven road, fishtailing almost out of control. They head wildly for the bridge bouncing and swaying and then girders suddenly flash past in a blur and a roar and Manning falls forward as Sheldon hits the brakes locking the wheels and burning rubber taking the turn after the bridge in a four-wheel drift and heading up the south riverside road. The rainshower clears; pale sunlight filters down; the road steams; the air is full of the smell of dampened dust.

A little later: 'Where are we going?' Neal asks.

'Anywhere,' says Sheldon. 'Any bloody where.'

His driving quietens and they turn more slowly from street to street, heading further south. The buildings are very old, here, with more elaborate and decoratively embellished façades, unlike the unitized simplicity of northside.

But the decay is far worse. Many structures have collapsed in on themselves, spilling out into the street.

'Badly built,' Neal says. 'Not strong enough.'

'They were built better than our zone,' Manning contradicts him. 'But they're much older. Our buildings will soon be like this. Broken down.'

'No, Oh no. Not like this.'

'Yeah,' Sheldon cuts in, 'sure, they fall down, boom, people killed, blood everywhere.' He laughs. Dressed wildly in scarlet cape and trousers, Sheldon's fantasy world overlaps reality, often encompassing people round him in everyday life. His dreams are as wild as his driving; often he finds it hard to distinguish between them and his function as gang leader.

Neal, intelligent but introverted and lacking imagination, is by his dullness a complementary personality and perfect companion.

'Nothing lasts for ever, Neal,' Manning persists. 'Not even our city.'

'It'll last, so long as I need it.'

'It won't, Neal. Northside buildings are already nearly falling down.'

Neal turns angrily in his seat. 'I know what I know,

Manning, and none of your arguing's going to change that. We've all had enough of it.'

'All I tell you is facts.'

They drive on in silence. Ahead, the buildings end in total collapse; a heap of rubble dotted with vegetation blocks the road completely. The asphalt is split in a maze of weed-choked cracks.

'Dead,' says Sheldon. He laughs, for no reason. 'City's lost its life blood.' He stops the car.

Neal fidgets uneasily. 'Why not go back now?' he says, looking away from the ruins. 'Turn round, Sheldon.'

Sheldon shrugs and U-turns.

'It *will* end like that,' Manning murmurs as they drive away from the ruins.

They have almost reached the bridge again when Sheldon brakes violently and jumps out of the car before it stops. He runs along the broken pavement with scarlet cape flapping behind him.

Neal looks around, confused. Manning points at the bridge. A girl is standing in the middle of the span, a hundred yards away. She is tall, thin, blonde. She turns warily, sees Sheldon and tenses ready to run. But the bridge is like a cage. She looks up and its iron girder frame stretches each side and above, marking grey shadow patterns on the road.

Sheldon is coming nearer. She panics and jumps on to the parapet, climbing from one rusty metal strut to the next, heading blindly for the top.

Sheldon follows her up. Neal and Manning get out of the car and walk closer, watching the two figures silhouetted against the pale sky. Neal says nothing; he seems upset.

The girl stops when she reaches the top, clinging to a strut high over the road, waiting, frozen. Sheldon advances, taking flamboyant risks, swinging carelessly up to her, never looking away from her. She flinches but is too scared to resist as he picks her up, balancing dangerously in the wind. He climbs down, carrying her on his arm.

Ignoring Manning and Neal he runs back to the car with the girl, puts her in the passenger seat and starts the engine. He accelerates past them, the girl beside him. 'New blood!' he shouts, skidding round the corner and across the bridge, back to northside, leaving Neal and Manning watching him go.

Long afterwards, Manning retains an image of the frightened girl instinctively burying her face in Sheldon's shoulder.

'Another girl,' Neal says dully. He grimaces. 'I must go back to the workshop.'

'No.' Manning catches hold of his arm. Neal's workshop – a converted garage – is the youth's retreat where he hides when under any kind of stress, taking refuge in a jungle of cars and machines. 'Come with me. I'm going to see your grandfather. Wickens. He has something to tell me.'

'But I got to work . . .' Their eyes meet, Neal looks away. 'Shit, Manning.'

They walk back over the bridge together, dwarfed by its size.

Wickens

Wickens's house stands on a hillside above rusting, overgrown dockyard cranes and warehouses, a dismal vista of machinery collapsing slowly into the stagnant river. The house is at the edge of what was once an exclusive suburb of self-contained houses crowded together, each with its its own garden patch. But what was a luxury in overpopulated times is now an absurdity; no one lives any more in the tiny-roomed, cramped houses overgrown with weeds. Wickens remains there in isolation.

His house stands apart, modified and rebuilt, a confused amalgam of architecture. Sections have been added over the years. Heavy concrete slabs abut tinted plastic panels and deep, floating windows. Turrets and domes sprout from the gabled roof. Neo-gargoyles glare down over stairs curling up the east wall to a rooftop patio.

But the panels are dented, the windows broken and boarded up, the steps have collapsed and the walls have subsided. The patchwork structure has aged with its occupier.

Neal and Manning walk in through the open front door and across peeling floor tiles into the kitchen. The smell is damp and foul. Wickens stands surrounded by empty packs and wrappers littering the floor and piled up round the cooker, where he is heating a meal. Dim light filters down through a high, narrow window.

He glances round at them, looks from one to the other, and turns back to his meal. He lifts vakpaks clumsily off the cooker and dumps them on a tray encrusted with food remnants. Manning steps back as the old man shuffles past without looking up. 'Food there. If you want it,' he mutters.

Manning leaves two packs to heat and follows Neal and the old man into the front room. Most windows are boarded up, admitting only cracks of light. The roof has fallen in one side and debris litters the damp-stained floor, where broken furniture is overturned on the tattered foam carpet.

Wickens sits hunched over his food by one of the few unbroken windows. It is raining, and water droplets snake down the outside of the glass, blurring the view of the river and dockyards at the bottom of the hill.

Wickens eats with nervous, jerky movements, digging his fingers into the breakfast paste, snatching mouthfuls of it from the foil tray. 'So why've you come?'

Manning sits down on a chair opposite; behind him, Neal sits half hidden on the floor by the door. 'Our talk this morning on the roof . . .' Manning begins.

'Not you, not you. Neal. Come out where I can see you, damn it. Why've you come? If to visit . . .'

Resentfully, Neal shifts forward. 'Manning brought me.'

'If you've got anything to add, about what you said this morning, Neal can hear it too,' Manning interjects.

'Ain't got nothing to say, not to you, Manning, so long

as you mix with his kind.' He gestures at Neal. 'I gave up years ago.'

'What do you mean, old man?' Neal says, scowling.

'Keep out of this.'

'Out of what?'

Wickens pushes his food aside and starts hauling himself up out of his chair. 'Don't know why you came here. You know you ain't welcome. Bad as the rest of 'em, sub-literate, don't know what you are, what you're doing, where you're going, call yourself grandson, hell, you ain't my grandson . . .'

'If you're on to another lecture . . .'

'Wouldn't have to lecture, if you'd listen. Look around and see sense, how it's dying, no more kids, no one's interested. Dying out, and it's your fault. You and the rest.'

'I listen, Wickens. I don't hear anything.'

'Course you don't. Never will. Tell you, I've given up, with your kind, trying to show you. But there's nothing'll show you, except force maybe. Force you out of the rut. A purge, dammit, that's what . . .'

Neal stands up, agitated, hands clenched, stepping forward. 'I told you,' he cuts in, voice tight and shrill, 'I told you old man, don't lecture me! All my life you been telling me I'm no good and not what you want. All my life you been saying there ain't nothing in me, things're falling apart. But it ain't going to change. Never. One day you'll push too hard, then someone'll get mad, and finish you for *good*.'

'Neal, he's right . . .' Manning begins.

'Leave me *be*, damn you Manning!' Neal is wild eyed, looking trapped, like someone surrounded. 'Get away, get away and leave me *be*!'

'Don't speak that way,' Wickens says, moving forward angrily. 'Not to me in my home.'

Neal is trembling. 'Stupid old man! Stupid, stupid, stupid . . .'

The muscles in Wickens's face are tensed rigid under the loose, flabby skin. He steps forward, bringing up his hands to clutch at Neal's throat. 'Child! you don't know, you'll never know, I've already taken steps, soon you'll be *made* to do what's good for you.'

Neal steps backward. He trips and falls. Wickens advances on him; he scrambles on to his feet. 'Get off, get off!' he shouts, hands moving over the wall behind him, fingers seeming to search for something to hold on to.

Then he lunges forward suddenly, butting Wickens in the stomach. The old man collapses on the floor, groaning. Neal hesitates, then bolts out of the room, away and down the road.

Manning pauses. It is suddenly quiet and still; all he can hear is Wickens's groaning, getting fainter. He bends over the old man who is lying eyes open, face up, on the floor.

'Wickens?' He shakes him. 'Neal's gone. But I want to know. What have you done? How are you forcing them out of the city? What have you done, the last two months?'

The old man is staring up but his eyes are focused somewhere behind Manning. He mutters half syllables, gasps for breath and starts pulling himself up, groping past Manning. He stands unsteadily in the middle of the room.

'Tell me what you've done, Wickens.'

The old man stumbles into the kitchen. Manning's breakfast packs are still on the cooker; Wickens hits out at the tinfoil trays and they fall sizzling into a heap of empty food wrappers on the floor. Then he collapses on to the grimy plastic tiles, eyes falling shut, muscles limp, breathing slowly.

Manning sighs. For a while, Wickens will be unreachable. When he comes out of it, he may never remember what he has done.

The Workshop

Outside, the rain is clearing. Manning walks back down the still-wet road, heading for Neal's workshop, reasoning that that is where the youth will have gone. It is midmorning, but the city lies as quiet as ever. Two seagulls wheeling slowly over the slow, grey river are the only signs of movement.

Rounding a corner, Manning sees something in the road ahead and walks closer, bending down to look at it. It is a dog lying mangled, dissected as though someone had cut it open looking for something inside it. Now it is dead. Neal's knife lies still plunged in the corpse where he finally killed it in frustration.

Manning frowns and walks past.

The workshop is on the ground floor of a multi-storey garage. Already Neal is busy in it; sounds of power tools alternate with the urgent revving of a car engine. Manning peers between a pair of double sliding doors. Inside is a litter of equipment and machines; the hundred feet by hundred feet floorspace is cluttered with a miscellany of twentieth-century engineering technology, grey metal gleaming in shadowless light shed by a ceiling of glow panels.

Against the walls are stacks of steel sheets, a hydraulic press, car frames, an excavator shovel, boxes of parts and drums wound with heavy chain. There are stacks of cogwheels; heaps of levers, tools and bolts; shelves piled with cable, switches and solid state control systems. Overhead rails carry a mobile hoist. A two-man helicopter crouches incongruously beside a giant ship's propeller in one corner.

This is Neal's retreat, stocked with pieces painstakingly gathered from all over the city. Dwarfed by the clutter of plastic and metal, he works on a car chassis, sliding under it, making adjustments, checking alignments. He slithers out and into the driving seat in one smooth, flowing movement, not noticing Manning enter the workshop until he appears from behind a stack of motor tyres.

Neal looks up. He lets the car engine slow to idling speed. 'What do you want? What are you doing in here?'

'I want to ask you something.'

Neal turns away, uninterested.

'I just want to know. If Wickens ever told you about his plan, his idea of forcing people out of the city. Has he done anything? Or is it just in his mind, another idea he'll never put into practice?'

'What do you care, Manning? You want us out of the city, too.'

'Yes. But Wickens is half crazy. He's dangerous.'

Neal sighs. 'He'd never say anything to me, Manning. He hates my guts. Now leave me alone.'

Manning turns and walks to the door. 'It's more important than you think.'

'Not to me. Not to us. We're not worried. We're city dwellers, he can't shift us. City dwellers, ain't nothing can change that.'

A Man and Woman

Like all of them, the apartment block is slowly falling to pieces. Its heavy, square-patterned façade is dirt-blackened, soot-streaked, windows broken, concrete cracked. The sections of wall are edging apart from one another.

Only one of the hundreds of two-room apartments is still lived in. The front room is small, square, low-ceilinged, and drab. The walls have yellowed and the pattern of the plastic floor covering is obliterated with dirt. Cheap plastic cups and bowls are stacked in a doorless cupboard. A broken clock stands half hidden by ragged curtaining drawn across the window. There are two upright moulded-plastic chairs either side of a moulded-plastic table – no other furniture.

A man is sitting on one of the chairs.

He is in his late forties, but his wrinkled, sweat-stained face is ageless. His chair is tilted back on two legs, his arms stretched flat out on the table top, shirt sleeves rolled up exposing black body hairs lying limply on his grey skin. He breathes slowly, chin on chest, dozing quietly, mind empty. The only sound is of the chair creaking with each slow exhalation.

Unnoticed, a fly is crawling slowly up over the hairs on one of his arms.

Taking slow, small steps, a woman enters, carpet slippers scraping over the dirty floor. She pauses, dimly scanning the familiar scene, breathing with difficulty, her sagging stomach painfully rising and falling. She brushes her tangled hair out of her face and continues to the window, stooped forward, mouth slack. She pulls the curtain aside and peers out.

Disturbed by her, the man rouses himself. His eyes open a crack and he swallows slowly. But he makes no movement. The fly still crawls on his arm.

He licks his cracked lips with a grey tongue. 'What – What –?'

The woman nods slowly toward something outside. 'Coming here.'

The man lets his chair fall slowly forward on to its front legs. He leans to the window, blinking and peering down. Together they watch Manning walking to the apartment building, until he disappears from view, entering through the main doors out of sight below.

The man frowns, fingering the thick skin of his face. The woman scowls. She shakes her head from side to side. It is a month since she last went out scavenging for food; she has been indoors ever since. The man cannot remember the last time he left the building. They have few friends, fewer visitors.

Faintly at first, they hear Manning's footsteps as he climbs the echoing stairwell.

Finally they hear him knock on the apartment door.

The woman hesitates, turning and shuffling out of the room, through the adjoining kitchenette. She opens the door a little and peers out; her eyes meet Manning's.

'Let me in,' he says.

He pushes the door and she reluctantly backs away, leaving space for him to squeeze past her. He walks through the sordid little kitchenette and the man looks round, blinking in the dim light, as Manning enters the living room.

The woman shuffles up behind, and shuts the door.

'I've come about Wickens,' Manning says.

The man frowns, leaning slowly forward. 'Eh?'

'About Wickens.'

He pauses, scratching stubble on his cheeks. 'Wickens? That – that's me. My name. I'm Wickens.' He seems confused.

'Not you, your father. Old man Wickens.'

'Old man Wickens. Ah.'

There is a short pause.

'Have you seen him?' Manning persists. 'Has he mentioned anything about . . . about the city?'

The man looks at the woman; she looks dumbly back at him. He coughs roughly and spits on the floor. 'Seen him, yes. A month, maybe three months back. Came here wanting me help him, something, don't know. Monorail, eight blocks up . . .' He trails off, squinting at Manning. 'Who you, what you want, anyhow? What doing coming here, me . . .'

'The monorail, the east line?'

'*I* know him,' the woman says. 'Seen him. With kids.'

'You mean the military warehouse? Wickens wanted you to go with him?'

'Kids, don't want none of *them*. Son of mine, no-good bastard, you go round with him eh? You piss-off, better go get out, go on you . . .'

The man heaves himself forward out of his chair, gasping and grunting. Manning steps back, calm and expressionless. 'It's got to be the military warehouse,' he says, glancing at the woman. She bares her teeth, peering up at him, her mouth twisted oddly.

They both stare blankly after Manning, as he steps quickly out.

Manning walks along the rusted steel monorail track, wind whipping at his clothes, clouds speeding overhead. The military warehouse is a favourite scavenging ground for youths; its barbed-wire barricades and automatic sentries have long since been disarmed and it lies wide open, stocked with machine parts, heavy vehicles, guns and ammunition. If Wickens had wanted help from his son to plunder the warehouse, his talk of using force would make more sense.

The elevated track curves round past rows of residential balconies and down a steep incline. Manning sees the squat warehouse ahead; but in between, on the monorail itself, two figures are walking away from him.

He stops and gropes inside his coat for his old pair of binoculars. When he focuses on the figures he sees it is Sheldon in his scarlet cape and the blonde girl; the youth captured on the iron bridge.

Manning watches as they stop and climb down a service ladder over the edge of the rail. He lowers his binoculars and thoughtfully walks nearer, finally breaking into a run.

The ladder leads down to an inspection platform slung under the concrete monorail arch. Manning creeps forward and peers over the edge. The ironwork platform is a secluded haven walled in by buildings either side and roofed by the track above. Sheldon is huddled there with the girl, undressing her with clumsy, fumbling motions as if his fingers are numb. As the shirt falls away from her dirt-smeared skin she presses herself to him, sheltering from the wind; but when he kisses her she responds passively, enduring him with resigned acceptance. Her tangled hair blows in her face; she makes no move to push it aside.

Sheldon caresses her breasts mechanically, unfeelingly and she slumps back under him, waiting. Their love-making is a soulless ritual, lacking meaning or emotion, motivated by curiosity in the absence of desire. Sheldon does what he feels he is supposed to do – what, perhaps, he once had a dream about – and he does not understand what he is doing. The procreative instincts have died.

The girl is naked, now, lying on her back, unresponsive as Sheldon touches her body, prodding her like a coroner performing an examination.

But then, unexpectedly, she opens her eyes. At once she sees Manning, peering down at her.

She cries out – a flat, unformed sound half lost in the wind – and Sheldon looks up, first confused, then angry.

Without understanding why, Manning panics. At once he feels caught out, discovered, trapped, guilty. He jumps up, hesitates, then runs clumsily along the monorail, his battered shoes coming off his feet, his coat billowing behind him like a great grey sail. He glances back and sees them climbing on to the rail after him. Ahead is another ladder to the ground. He swings down it, rips his coat, slips and tumbles from rung to rung. Sheldon and the girl shout down at him, words lost in the rushing wind. Rain starts blowing in sheets of fine spray; Manning slips and falls in a shower of rust. He lands painfully, jumps up and runs. They follow him down the ladder. The rain comes in heavier droplets painting pale streaks in the grime on the girl's naked back. Manning runs on blindly ahead stumbling past debris-littered abandoned cinemas and uncompleted building projects overgrown with weeds, across parks littered with bricks and concrete sections, under peeling façades of rotting advertising hoardings. Rain pours down in a grey curtain; behind it, office blocks rear up blanking off all escape routes, walling him in. His feet slap down in the rain, through puddles and soggy mud. His shoes are gone. His heels and insteps bleed from rusty cans and glass fragments. Breath comes short, a cramped pain. His sight blurs. Fatigue grabs at his limbs. He is lost in a grey ocean. Soot-blackened brickwork and broken windows move before him in unending procession. Long streets stretch to infinity.

When he finds himself outside the library he runs in unthinkingly, near collapse, hands groping for the bookshelves to keep himself upright. Water pours down his face and off his clothes. He stumbles through the dim aisles and finds his rough bed.

He sinks down on it, straight into sleep.

Carole

When Manning awakes, the girl is there.

He sees her standing in dim evening light filtering through one of the curtained library windows. He lies still, watching her, and slowly she walks over to where he is slumped, soaking wet, feet smeared with blood, on his bed of torn paper.

'I waited for you to wake up,' she says quietly. 'It's evening now. You slept through all afternoon.'

Manning sits up slowly, nervously, feeling hemmed in. He shivers, clutching his arms round himself. His muscles ache. His skin is ice cold.

'Are you alone here?' he asks.

She nods slowly. 'I ran from Sheldon.'

'Why? Because of . . . of what I saw?'

She shakes her head, faintly amused. 'I don't like him. He takes. I need help. I'm from outside, another centre, it died out. I'm alone.' She pauses, studying him. Her face is pale, like her hair. 'My name is Carole. I've found food.' She hands him cold food packs. He takes them warily, breaking the plastic seals and gobbling the uncooked contents, keeping his eyes on her all the time.

'Are they all like Sheldon, Manning?'

'What?'

'Cold, like him. Is everyone? You?'

'I don't know.'

'Why did you run, that way? Afraid?'

He looks away, confused, remembering the sudden

guilt of being discovered seeing Sheldon and the girl together.

'Who *are* you, Manning?'

He sighs. 'I wasn't born here. Didn't know my parents. Man called Wickens found me abandoned near his house; I was two. He looked after me. I grew up here in the library. Mostly on my own, always on my own, moving around. I don't know, I look at as many books as I can but it's hard, I . . . don't think much about myself.' He looked away from the girl, in sudden confusion.

'This place is a library?'

'No one uses it now.'

'Why should they?'

'It can answer questions.'

'I haven't got any questions.'

Manning shakes his head. 'Like the rest. You aren't interested. You're never interested.' He glances briefly at her. 'Better off with Sheldon.'

She looks directly at him and he feels trapped, unable to look away, wishing she'd left him alone. 'I don't like Sheldon,' she says. 'I told you. With him I get used, like he uses his car.'

Manning tries to fight down his feelings of compassion, aroused by the way that, like him, she doesn't fit with the other city dwellers.

She frowns. 'Please let me stay here with you.'

He doesn't answer. She stands up, walks over to him, stands close facing him, putting her hands on his shoulders. He stands stiff and cold, trying not to look at her. Her breath is on his face. 'Please?'

Half-heartedly, he raises his hand and places it fumblingly round her waist. 'You can stay if you really want to.'

She frowns. 'They say you think you know a lot. I thought you'd be nicer to me.'

He shrugs.

'You know a lot about people, Manning; haven't you ever known someone as a person, face to face? Always cut yourself off, haven't you, hiding here?'

He nods weakly. She studies his face, stroking it, and a fraction at a time he finds himself relaxing.

But the moment of peace and stillness is shattered by sudden noise from outside.

The Cache

At once alert, Manning grips her hand and hurries her out of the library down the front steps and behind one of the pillars. It is almost dark outside.

The noise rises from a distant growl to an angry, shattering, crackling roar as more than thirty cars swarm round the corner and stop outside the library in ragged formation. Dust and exhaust fumes rise in the blinding headlamp glare glinting on the metal frames of the cars and their massive engines.

Manning holds Carole back behind the thick pillar, out of sight of the youths running from their cars and up the front steps. Squinting against the white brilliance, Manning sees they carry rifles, grenades, flame throwers, and hand weapons. Shouts cut across the rumble of the idling car engines as the youths charge into the library firing at random.

Others run down the street shouting and smashing windows, throwing smoke bombs and screaming wildly. The smoke billows and drifts in thick clouds.

The youths run back out of the library. Sheldon, leading them, pauses on the steps. 'Not here,' he shouts. 'But we'll find him. We'll get him, get his blood!' They cheer. 'The square!' he screams, 'to the square!'

He jumps into the leading car and takes off down the street, cloak blowing scarlet out behind him. The rest of the pack follow; slowly the noise dies away.

Manning blinks. His vision is a blur of swimming after images. His ears are buzzing, hands trembling. He walks down the steps pulling Carole after him.

'Got to get to the town square.'

'Are they hunting you because I ran to you from Sheldon?'

'Perhaps that started it. But it's been building up to this, the last month. They have to have a start for their riots. This time it's me.'

Ahead they can hear shouts and explosions, car engines revving, machine-guns hammering. Manning, still dazed, stumbles toward the noise, pale but determined.

'Why, Manning? Why is this happening?'

'Riot night. The only outlet. They don't take sides, it's not like that, they fight at random, smash buildings, each other, anything they feel like doing, they do it.'

'Why are we going where they're fighting?'

'Old Man Wickens. He talked a lot about using force. If he's going to, it'll be tonight. Seeing them riot drives him mad. He'll get them out of the city any way he can. He can't bear it being so purposeless.'

He pushes her ahead of him into the entrance hall of an apartment block. In some previous riot it has been gutted, walls smashed in in places, bannisters lying in a twisted tangle at the bottom of the stairwell. Patches of moonlight are scattered at random in the darkness.

They climb to the fifth floor and feel their way along a dark corridor. Manning pauses. 'There's a chance that if Wickens has heard the riot, he's come here. He used to use this place.'

Motioning her silent, he picks up a lump of broken concrete and creeps along the corridor, counting the doors as he goes. He pauses, then pushes in through the seventh door.

But inside, the room is empty. A broken desk and overturned chair lie coated in dust in the moonlight by the window. Papers litter the floor.

Manning sighs and drops the lump of concrete.

'The papers,' Carole says, picking up some of the sheets. 'Won't they mean anything?'

'No. They must date back to when he wrote here, years ago.'

Manning looks out of the window. It gives a good view

of the square. Bursts of gunfire alternate with flashes of light from car headlamps. Engines roar and there is the distant, echoing sound of screaming tyres.

Manning sees a sheet of paper still in the typewriter on the desk. He pulls the sheet out; there is just enough light from the window for him to read.

'Page one of a thesis,' he reads aloud, '"The Rise and Fall of the City, the death of Civilized Existence".' He drops the paper on the floor. 'By R. A. Wickens. Written five years ago.'

But Carole isn't listening. She has wandered into the adjoining room. 'Come in here,' she calls. 'Tell me what this is.'

He follows her in but stops in the doorway.

Petrol cans are stacked in the shadows, filling the room from floor to ceiling. In one corner is a small detonator. Manning frowns, stepping slowly forward, looking round in disbelief. He looks at the detonator. 'Radio controlled,' he says slowly. 'Enough to make a small blast, spread the burning petrol . . .'

'You mean he can blow this up?'

'From wherever he is. This, and the others he must have set up. Other caches. It's so obvious, if you think like Wickens. Choose the simplest means. Get people out by destroying their homes. Destroy the whole centre.' Manning wipes his hand across his forehead. 'It's taken him the last two months to do all this. The crazy old man.'

He stands motionless for a moment; then he turns and catches hold of her hand. 'We can still find him and stop him setting everything off, killing people and destroying everything.'

She runs back down the corridor after him, down the stairs and into the street.

On the edge of the centre, away from the beginnings of the riot in the town square, Wickens's house stands silent, windows dark, empty and deserted. Manning pauses outside, breathing hard. Carole leans on him, exhausted from the run from the town square. 'Maybe he's in there asleep,' she says.

'Too early, he's probably out. But we'll check.' Manning walks into the house, followed by the girl. It is absolutely still and almost completely dark, faint moonlight piercing the cracks between the boards covering the broken windows.

Manning wanders through the house, but Wickens is not there. He turns, about to leave, but at that moment catches sight of a grey shape leaping at him from the shadows. He twists to one side, but hands grapple for him and close on his throat; he falls on his back gasping and choking. They struggle together on the floor and roll into a patch of moonlight and only then does he realize that it is not Wickens but Neal, hate-faced and wide-eyed, who jumped on him without warning.

Slowly the youth's staring eyes focus on Manning; slowly, reluctantly, he relaxes his grip. Suddenly he pulls away, cursing. 'You bastard, Manning, I don't want you. I want the old man.'

Manning scrambles up. 'Wickens? You wanted to kill Wickens?'

'Time to settle the score, get back at him for all the times he's been at me, pushing me, lecturing me . . .'

'That's not enough of a reason.'

'Fuck your reasons, Manning. Riot night. Tonight I kill him.' Neal turns and walks to the door. 'I'm going to find him. Now.' He vanishes outside, running off into the night.

Shaken by the sudden attack, Manning walks to the front door and looks out.

'It all comes out of them. Even someone dull like Neal. Transformed.'

'He's Wickens's son?' asks Carole.

'His grandson. The old man brought him up, tried to save him from being like the rest, but all it did was make Neal hate him and hate learning anything. Fighting the boy's will to be like his friends was like fighting evolution. Or devolution.' Manning sighs. 'Let's get back to the square. Our last chance is to find Wickens there.'

The square is blazing with light and roaring with sound. Running figures dive for cover under searchlight beams and exploding shells. Machine-gun fire sweeps overhead. The roads and the central area of overgrown vegetation are crisscrossed with shifting beams of light.

Crouched in an alley near the town hall, Manning and Carole watch the scene, huddled together against the wall. A cluster of tactical rockets shoot overhead, gushing smoke and lighting the square with yellow glare. But the guidance systems are faulty and the small missiles waver erratically and spin down at random, impacting at the base of an office building. Fireballs bloom. The ground shudders and shudders again as the building collapses with a roar, falling in on itself. Someone near Manning is laughing hysterically.

'It's worse than ever before,' he shouts to her above the noise. 'They must have found a whole arsenal hidden somewhere.'

Through clouds of smoke and dust a makeshift armoured vehicle is making its way insect-like into the square, guns on continuous automatic, shattering windows and walls. Searchlights converge on it. Bullets slam against its armoured shell, hammering off the curved metal plating. Suddenly the vehicle erupts in flames, firing distress signals and magnesium flares over the square: blazing red, green and white. Through it all comes the sound of screaming.

'Almost out of control,' Manning says. 'Before, they've managed somehow to keep it within limits, but this . . .'

Behind him, Carole has turned away, covering her ears against the insistent gunfire and explosions. But Manning, like a murder witness, stares compulsively, drawn to the scene, watching in horrified fascination.

In the square, a tank rumbles forward, crushing abandoned cars littering the street. Then it hits a mine and the arena blazes yellow. The pounding thump of the explosion echoes and re-echoes. The blast overturns the tank, smashing it through a supermart store front. For a long moment, the building balances, half of its structure broken away. Then the ground-floor walls cave in and the upper storeys settle in a rushing, rumbling cascade of concrete and brick dust. Running figures converge on the ruins.

Manning turns and shouts in Carole's ear: 'Not safe here. Town hall. Follow me.' They dodge through back streets, pausing in shadowy doorways while youths in army vehicles thunder past yelling and throwing grenades into shop windows. Manning has lost hope of finding Wickens and of stopping the riot. The only thing he can do is seek safety until it is all over.

Under the sky flashing with rockets and signal flares stands the town hall, dark, silent and solid, square and heavy. Manning is heading for the front steps with Carole behind him when a new noise from up and behind makes him stop and look.

A helicopter is descending, engine roaring, rotors shimmering in the searchlight beams aimed up at it from the square.

Manning remembers seeing the machine in Neal's workshop. But he never dreamed the youth could ever discover how to get it to work and how to fly it. He grimaces at the irony; Wickens himself probably supplied the knowledge, directly or indirectly, in the first place.

Now the helicopter is swooping low, its landing lights ablaze, firing at unprotected figures running for cover in the square. Manning glimpses Sheldon piloting it, Neal beside him; it lifts, wobbles, turns erratically, then sideslips out of control as gunfire strikes one of the rotors.

The helicopter falls, lights still on; it smashes down on

youths running beneath. Fuel tanks explode and fire boils over the ground. Manning sees Sheldon running, scarlet cape ablaze with yellow flames, screaming through the night, smashing through a store window and falling dying in a heap of empty food wrappers. Neal is flat on the ground under the broken machine; fire swallows him. All over the square, people are converging on the scene. Gunfire ceases. Cars are abandoned. Figures start gathering round. All is silent; the roaring of flames is the only remaining sound.

At first, no one notices as Wickens steps out of the main town hall doors.

Manning is the first to see the thin, hunched figure waiting at the top of the front steps, overlooking the square. Manning runs up silently and with a gasp lunges forward and fells Wickens.

'The radio transmitter,' he cries, 'to trigger the explosives. Where is it? Give it to me!'

The old man is stunned by his fall. He groans and tries to focus his eyes. Then he sees it is Manning. He smiles slowly and painfully. 'Nothing – nothing you can do,' he croaks. 'Pre-set. Any time now. Back at my house. Did you think I'd chance . . .' His voice trails off. His old eyes fall shut.

Manning stands up. 'If we can reach his house in time, and find the trigger . . .'

His words are cut off as, simultaneously over the city, buildings explode and fire roars boiling over them. Soon the whole sky is yellow with flames.

City Death

It is dawn; Manning and Carole stand alone in the fire-blackened square.

The fire has swept over the whole zone, burning throughout the night. Homes have been gutted, forcing men and women who had not ventured out for months to take refuge in the streets. Buildings have collapsed. There is no water or electricity. Food has almost all been incinerated. More than three-quarters of the population has been killed as a result of the riots and the flames. Wickens, Neal, and Sheldon are all dead.

Manning and Carole, having taken refuge overnight in the fire-proof, impregnable town hall vaults, walk amongst the still smouldering debris and gutted buildings. They say nothing, staring sadly about them.

The square is bordered by mere mounds of tumbled concrete where buildings had once stood; the rubble has spilled across the surface of the road, engulfing twisted, ruined vehicles.

Manning feels suddenly lost and isolated. Carole has started crying. She turns away from the desolate destruction as they walk through the empty streets.

Men and women here and there sit blankly in front of the rubble of their former homes. They seem uninterested when Manning tries to get them to come with him, out of the city. Two youths, trying to turn a car back on its wheels, want only to drive home. A blind man, trying vainly to get into a store blocked by a mass of fallen brickwork, wants help to climb over the debris. They cannot sway his single-minded determination.

Still alone together, Manning and Carole pass the library building. Fire-proof, it was one of the few to escape unburnt. Manning pauses, wanting to go back into it among the books again in the semi-darkness. Already he is getting accustomed to the ruined skyline, the broken buildings, still somehow solid, reassuring, lying in great heaps on all sides.

He sighs. 'Wickens was wrong. Destruction isn't enough to break the bonds. Man and city . . . even this won't force people out.'

'*I* don't want to go,' she says.

But together, forcing themselves, they walk slowly on along the street, heading south, not looking back. Ahead are the city limits. Beyond, the countryside.

Behind them, the city is dead.